Vampires

Vampires

A HANDBOOK OF
HISTORY & LORE
OF THE **UNDEAD**

Agnes Hollyhock

castle

Table of Contents

Introduction

The line between life and death is one of the great mysteries that has inspired awe and fear in humanity since before the dawn of civilization. Funeral rites may be the first human culture ever developed, and stories about the netherworld and its denizens stretch back across the campfires of history. Though contemplating the transformation of the soul after death provokes anxiety, the idea that the dead might return from their sunless land to steal the vitality of the living has terrorized our collective consciousness with unique staying power.

Vampires, in all their many forms, have gone from being spoken of in hushed voices and recorded in monster-hunting manuals to being an extremely popular (and profitable) feature of modern media. The cultural obsession that arguably began with John William Polidori's novella *The Vampyre* was renewed for modern audiences by Anne Rice's The Vampire Chronicles, the television show *Buffy the Vampire Slayer*, and the *Vampire: The Masquerade* video game. Most of us have probably engaged with the legend of the vampire in some way, whether you dressed up as Dracula for Halloween, played *Castlevania*, or sang the vampire anthem "Total Eclipse of the Heart" at karaoke.

While fewer people today believe in literal vampires than they did before the Age of Enlightenment, vampires stand in as a metaphor for a variety of concepts and experiences. Vampire stories have been viewed as a lens for exploring women's sexuality, LGBTQ+ identity, religious taboos, HIV and other stigmatized diseases, and intergenerational trauma. In some stories, vampires are villains, while in others, they are sympathetic underdogs who fight against their predatory natures, reminding us that we can always choose to do better. Vampires have also come to epitomize the goth aesthetic, leading to the establishment of live role-play communities, themed nightclubs, and dedicated fashion subcultures.

However, under the mountains of modern vampire media and analysis now available, much has been forgotten. The folktales, history, and occult secrets of the vampire are even more surprising to us today because they do not neatly adhere to the vision of the "typical" vampire popularized in *Dracula* and subsequent imaginings. Most of us don't know why vampires can't abide garlic, or what kind of wood you would need to stake one with; we have forgotten that coins could harm vampires, and that some of them consume breath or energy, rather than blood. The fascinating science that tells us how the earliest vampire superstitions came to be is likewise hardly discussed. For those who wish to pull back the curtain and find out the lost secrets of vampire lore, I hope this book will offer an exciting starting point.

There are many ways to examine the history and lore of vampires, and integrating a historically rooted, cross-cultural view of the vampire will help us learn more about why humanity finds them so fascinating. Examining the evolution from the earliest bloodsucking demons in recorded history to today's popular depictions casts a wide net of possible vampiric creatures and lore to pull from.

While elements can be seen in folklore across the globe, the word *vampire* and many of its most associated attributes are directly linked to the European vampire (which originated in Slavic folklore). This depiction of a vampire is an undead

human risen from the grave, that has a corporeal body, is active at night, and feeds on the blood of living victims. These vampires can sometimes take an incorporeal or animal form, and are often thought to be weak to silver, garlic, and Catholic artifacts. Although some iteration of the Slavic vampire is what we most often see in media nowadays, other vampire-like creatures with roots in other cultures and areas liken vampires to demons or fey beings, rather than undead humans. Some are primarily incorporeal, others feed on living essences other than blood, and so forth.

Finally, I will note that any review of vampire lore will inevitably touch upon cultural practices that are no longer familiar to most readers. Premodern burial practices, violations thereof, and superstitions are discussed, which were often made the subject of mockery and paranoia as scientific advancement cast doubt on the existence of vampires. I encourage you to keep an open mind rather than judge people too harshly for their viewpoints, and where possible I include scientific notes explaining how rational people came to hold these beliefs in the first place. I also seek to avoid the pitfalls of the nineteenth-century literature that subtly presented vampires as dangerous, lustful foreigners who carried diseases, reinforcing the xenophobia of the period. Thankfully, these associations have faded somewhat in the popular imagination as new ideas of the vampire take root.

So, turn the page, and delve bravely into the myth of the vampire—who takes many forms, lives eternally, and dines on that which we hold most dear. Whether you believe in vampires yet or not, these monarchs of the night may take hold in your dreams . . .

What Is a Vampire?

I imagine that if you're picking up this book, you might already have an idea of what a vampire could be. These undead or demonic creatures of the night have evolved over their centuries of existence, and exactly what constitutes a vampire depends on who's telling the story. For the purposes of this book, I'll define the basics of what it means to be a vampire: the key attributes and biology of these iconic horror figures to help set up a base of knowledge for all the information that follows.

WHAT TO KNOW ABOUT VAMPIRES

The short and simple definition of a vampire that I will use for this book is an undead creature or powerful otherworldly entity that sustains itself on the living essence of humans or other creatures to survive. This essence can be—and most frequently is—blood, but psychic energy and essential life force are also things that vampires can feed on. With this definition in mind, the first thing you need to know about vampires is that they are hungry, and they are subject to this hunger in a way that mere mortals will never understand. They will not only slowly starve without a living creature to sustain them, but the agony of their hunger can also drive them to do despicable things.

There are many types of vampires that pop up in firsthand accounts, fiction, and oral traditions. Vampires have a storied history that is riddled with facts, fabrications, and folktales (that are often treated as fact). While there are many firsthand accounts, the menacing history of vampires recorded by

people who came before us often involves an undead creature inexplicably returning from the grave to torment their loved ones and community. Nowadays, vampires are treated predominantly as fictional characters, but their existence was very real to the people who made these claims, and each historical account has a palpable quality of mass hysteria that radiates off the page for modern readers despite the centuries that separate them from the original event.

Even now, there are some cultures and people who believe vampires to be legitimate, despite how unsubstantiated firsthand accounts and claims may be when examined under scientific scrutiny. These firsthand accounts (and therefore the root of vampires' legitimacy) can be explained away by modern science and medical knowledge. But retroactively explaining away vampires' existence doesn't stop superstitions from worming their way into the collective subconscious. Their enthralling horror is more than science can bear.

Additionally—aside from the staying power of vampire mythology, folklore, and superstitions—what I find most peculiar is the ubiquitous appearance of vampirism across cultures. How and why did so many cultures spontaneously decide upon the existence of a mystical creature traversing the night in search of living essences to feast on? We may never know the root truth of vampire origins, but I will certainly try to excavate a sliver of it through examining the historical accounts and folklore. Join me as I define what it means to be a vampire.

FOLKLORE AND THE POWER OF FEAR

Folklore and mythology are often used interchangeably. For the sake of this book, I'll boil down the differences to scope.

Mythology is something grand and sacred, more like a religion that deals with divinity and immortal cosmic beings.

Folktales, which are a prime component of folklore, are a collection of stories (usually based on superstitions) that are significantly smaller in scope and are usually tied to specific regions. They have mundane and everyday characters and are often passed word of mouth by people in the community.

Vampires show up a lot in both folklore and mythology, so it's important to differentiate between the two.

For vampires in folklore, the most widely referenced iteration of the vampire folktale was of the Eastern European vampires. People in those areas believed that the spirits of their dead lingered after they left their mortal bodies. These spirits were meant to be respected and catered to, which would result most of the time in the spirits moving on to the afterlife. However, improper burials or slights after death would often result in malevolent spirits, and sometimes (often alongside a plague or pandemic) these spirits would reinhabit their corpse and become vampire plagues on their community.

When Catholicism came to Eastern Europe, vampire folklore mixed with Catholic mythology. Eastern European folktales were adopted by the Catholic Church in part because vampires (while malevolent and terrifying) were clear evidence that there was an afterlife (and a proper and improper way to gain entry to it).

BIOLOGY OF THE UNDEAD

There are many types of vampires, but many people think of undead immortal blood drinkers whenever vampires are mentioned nowadays. These essential vampiric qualities have their root in misunderstood medical phenomena, and modern vampire enthusiasts and historians can tease out the fact behind the folklore.

To dissect this perception of the vampire, I'll begin by lightly examining seventeenth- and eighteenth-century Eastern European vampire folklore, where the initial vampire craze took off. There's evidence that certain Eastern European cultures believed in vampires as early as the ninth century, but the latter centuries are what helped popularize the folklore outside of its area of origin. Many of the attributes that we associate with vampires today come from the folklore of that time.

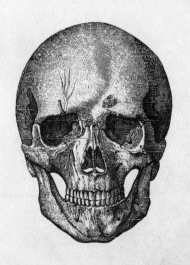

Most of the observations that I cite below have come from primary sources from seventeenth- and eighteenth-century Europe (and most "legitimate" sources were historical accounts from vampire hunters). With rudimentary medical knowledge of questionable quality, the rural communities that were ravaged by what they believed to be vampires (but was likely smallpox or another disease) would hire a vampire hunter to rid themselves of their vampire. These vampire hunters would investigate vampiric claims (usually with the town following them as a curious and fearful mob) and uncover a vampire in its coffin. They would make the following assumptions from their observations.

Undead: Vampires are most frequently seen as undead creatures than any other major vampire archetype. They're rarely born, but rather made by another vampire, and newly minted vampires are only vampires after they've perished. This belief has its roots in a lack of medical knowledge and the desire of the people to come to an understanding of

1) why people were wasting away from sicknesses they couldn't understand, and 2) why families were not only emotionally wounded by the loss of a loved one but frequently soon after claimed by the grave as well. Vampiric science, while debunked by many modern methodologies, made sense to the common people ravaged by unknown diseases that they had no knowledge on how to beat.

Immortality: Immortality and death are usually contradictory aspects, but immortal undead vampires return from the grave and stop aging from the day they die to the day a vampire hunter seeks to end them. Immortality was thought to have been achieved by vampires because when vampire hunters dug up suspected vampires (usually within thirty days of them being buried), their bodies did not appear to have decayed. Their hair and nails looked to have continued growing, and their skin might even appear ruddy or pink. These observations developed the folkloric belief that vampires did not age after death.

However, those bodies *were* decaying. Hair and nail growth were due to the slow desiccation of the rest of the body pulling the skin tighter around the skeleton. And a ruddy complexion was a result of blood pooling and beginning to decay once the heart stopped.

Blood: Blood was considered a vital life essence, but its biological purpose was not widely known when stories of blood-drinking monsters haunted Eastern European folklore. It wasn't until the 1900s that we even knew about the different blood types. For the rural residents of

Eastern Europe, blood was an important enigma of the human body. When vampire hunters threw off coffin lids, sometimes the suspected vampire would have ruddy cheeks (presumably from gorging on blood) and red liquid coming from their mouth (which rural residents assumed to be blood). What vampire hunters and the rural community thought to be blood was actually a sign that the corpse's insides were decomposing, and the gases created in that process would push blood and bile out of their mouths.

Fangs: Fangs are a common trait among undead vampires in Eastern Europe as well. Folklore would tell us that these fangs are used to drink blood. Firsthand accounts cite vampire fangs as being elongated rather than sporting sharp canine incisors. The medical reason behind this firsthand account is that the gum tissue recedes as the body decomposes, making the teeth appear longer and more pronounced.

While these traits do not appear on all vampires across all cultures, their ever-present existence helps us build a most-common vampire archetype and connect the facts as they were seen by the people who created the folklore but now with a keener eye and modern medical knowledge.

ICONIC HORROR FIGURES

Vampires' beginnings are very much one of fear—the prospect of a vampire at someone's window would be utterly terrifying to the people who truly believed that these creatures were real. Their modern pop-culture representations do not exclusively evoke the same feelings of terror in modern audiences, and many would willingly invite them into their rooms to watch them sleep (I'm looking at you, Twilight Saga, see page 165).

Modern fictional vampires are almost entirely divorced from the folklore and mythology that inspired the original characters in fiction (primarily Bram Stoker's *Dracula* and Joseph Sheridan Le Fanu's *Carmilla*). Although these initial characters were portrayed as equal parts alluring and terrifying, something about being young, beautiful, and powerful forever blotted out the popular perception that vampires were meant to be feared. While not the topic of this book, pop culture is its own type of folklore. What is pop culture if not popular stories—widely acknowledged as fictional—that play on our hopes and fears to help us solve whatever existential questions plague us at that time?

Vampires used to be superstitions debunkable with adequate medical knowledge. Thanks to pop culture's liberally creative interpretations of folklore, they can be a tool to help us tease out cultural trauma and existential questions.

As vampires enter and exit pop culture, their images tend to change. Like many things in the media, they emerge after a period of dormancy and their appearance is subsequently altered by the people who write stories about them. What a vampire represents has changed, but what follows are common themes that arise when vampire folklore inspires fiction.

Fear

Much of the fear that inspired vampire folklore was fear of disease and the unknowns that happen after death. That terror was often foisted onto the recently departed in the form of vampirism. There is also a connection between vampirism and the fear of invaders. Many of the key reports of vampirism are from the Austrian-occupying forces in

Eastern Europe. Vlad the Impaler (see page 92) earned his bloody reputation from defending his home in Wallachia (in modern-day Romania) from the Ottoman Empire. In modern fictional vampire stories, the fear comes from trying to defeat a nigh-insurmountable vampiric monster. These contemporary vampires are still creatures to be feared, but there are very few vampire stories (or monster stories in general) where the source of the audience's terror is not defeated by the protagonists.

Power

More so than the vampires of folklore, vampires in fiction are usually a symbol of power. The aristocratic vampire, a bloodsucking fiend with affluence and taste, sits well in the public consciousness. After all, they have all the time in the world, so why wouldn't they be wealthy and cultured? They symbolize generational wealth, infinite time, privilege, and influence. Their power can also be seen in their abilities, of which modern vampires can have many (including telepathy, telekinesis, accelerated healing, shapeshifting, mind control, and many more). Their ambition is the flip side of this coin—the price for all their power is the symbolic and literal blood of others on their hands. Latest versions of fictional vampires usually pose some version of the following question: What would you trade for power—compassion, empathy, your soul? For these vampires, the answer is often *yes*.

Romance and Sexuality

A vampire's primal hunger for blood aligns linguistically (and thematically, in most cases) to desire and arousal.

Many vampires of folklore would revisit their wives in death and the grieving widows were either happy or horrified in welcoming their undead husbands home. The yearning for blood also translates to a yearning for something taboo—whether that's coded toward desire in general, or that of the closeted feelings of LGBTQ+ people.

Classic pieces of vampire media (*Carmilla* and *Interview with the Vampire*) both have queer undertones during periods when queerness was stigmatized or even prosecuted. Some of vampires' many powers are their beautiful visages and irresistible nature, which can make people wonder, *Why resist?* Is it their own desires they're resisting, or is it easier to give in to something desired (yet forbidden) if it is an internal struggle they are bound to lose? Additionally, fictional vampires from the twenty-first century who keep their morals (a "good" vampire) will likely suppress their desire for blood and penchant for violence, which likely increased their appeal in the romance market.

Mortality and What It Means to Be Human

What would you do with all the time in the world? Study medicine? Perfect an art form? Lean into every hedonic desire? The allure of living forever and remaining young and beautiful for that eternity becomes increasingly more enticing as humans pack more and more into each hour of the day. Modern vampire media will often ask its cultural consumers what they would be willing to trade for forever. Is it worth giving up humanity in perpetuity to grow past human limits? Many vampires in more modern media (the previously mentioned "good" ones) struggle with being turned into monsters. The presence of their morality is sometimes alluded to as a soul. Themes in modern vampire stories usually beg the question of what it means to be human and what it means to be monstrous.

ENERGY AND PSYCHIC VAMPIRES

Alongside the bloodsucking vampires of legends are energy and psychic vampires. The definition for both energy and psychic vampires has changed over the centuries. Nowadays, energy vampires are usually talked about in conjunction with empaths. These humans are called vampires because they suck social and emotional energy from people they're close to, and this can be exhausting for empathetic people or people pleasers. Psychic vampires can be living or dead and leach life energy from their victims, usually in their sleep. They are equally as prevalent in the early folklore of vampires as their bloodier counterparts.

To understand psychic vampires, there are theories of the soul and body that must be understood first. Humans have three bodies: there is the conscious soul, the physical body, and the astral body.

The **soul** is loosely the consciousness of a person and is everything that makes you, you. The soul at any point can be attached to either of the two bodies that follow.

The **physical body** is what bloody vampires feed off—it consists of blood, muscles, and physical tissue that allow humans to move around in physical space.

The **astral body** is frequently attached to the physical body and expands to about a foot (30 cm) outside of the physical body. The astral body is leashed to the physical body but can also detach itself and move incorporeally through space and travel far distances, which is sometimes called astral projection, soul "traveling," or described as out-of-body experiences.

The astral body or the soul are what psychic vampires feed from.

Psychic vampires can use their astral body to travel great distances and consume the astral bodies of others, most often when they're sleeping. Psychic vampires can be living humans, or they could be the astral body of a deceased person exclusively sustaining their astral body on the energy of others. Victims of these feedings will sometimes see the visage of the psychic vampire looming over them while they're sleeping or see their presence haunting their dreams.

Victims cite most of these attacks happening between 3 and 5 a.m. and are usually accompanied by a sense of dread or paralysis of the physical body. Accounts of psychic vampirism reflect some of the firsthand reports of undead vampires in folklore—which include vampires coming to them in the night, sitting on their victim's chest, and draining them of energy.

Vampire History

Though the word "vampire" did not enter common parlance until 1746, when a French scholar published a treatise on cases of vampire hunts in Serbia and Poland, the creature's origins stretch much further back in history. This chapter offers a historical overview of the vampire's evolution in different regions, paying special attention to the key characteristics that sprang up or disappeared over time. Just as the vampire has changed, so too have the weapons used against them, though these are almost always items that are readily accessible to the common person.

FOLK BELIEFS ACROSS CULTURES

Vampires and their ilk have inspired a wide variety of folk practices across the world. The majority of these pertain to the prevention or destruction of vampires, such as burying corpses upside down or preparing stakes to impale them. These practices and others will be discussed further in the next section, where we will explore vampiric lore and abilities (see page 51). Others are geared toward providing protection from vampires and other undead spirits, such as hanging herb garlands around windows or burning onion skins over a young child.

There are also holidays and festivals that can claim the vampire as part of their purpose. The ancient Greek Anthesteria, and the Roman Feast of Lemuria that came after it, were both springtime festivals in which households would renew wards on their property to keep the dead out of their homes for another year. This was particularly important for the Romans, who believed that even a household god could die and become a vampiric spirit that drained its former charges!

Hundreds of years later, the winter Feast of Saint Andrew in Romania took on a similar role, as people in Eastern Europe worried that the dead were particularly likely to roam between November 30 and January 6 (Epiphany). People would spend Saint Andrew's Eve applying garlic to themselves, their homes, and their livestock to ward off vampires.

Several Asian holidays share a different association with vampires. The Hindu holiday of Diwali, for example, was thought not to repel vampires but in some sense to actually *create* them. Young women who died tragic deaths during Diwali were thought to be particularly likely to rise from their graves, bitter at the irony of their own misfortune. People were thus on guard against potential disaster striking during those most holy days of the year. Today, the Aswang Festival of the Philippines is named for that region's vampires (see page 35), but it is a modern invention in the vein of Halloween that celebrates the monsters of Filipino folktales. Though it is a merry occasion with carnivals and parades, many people recognize that it also helps keep alive the old superstitions about the dead.

FORGOTTEN ANCESTORS

Because vampires have existed in human mythology for millennia, and likely predate written language, identifying a single origin for the idea is impossible. However, there are common themes in vampire lore that are found across the earliest recorded examples, helping us to theorize what inspired early humans to believe in vampires.

Vampires in ancient Mesopotamia, Asia, and the Mediterranean were associated with owls—particularly screech owls. Some only took their names from these birds, while others were thought to have avian features or be able to transform into owls at will. These nocturnal birds clearly inspired unease, and their carnivorous nature may have inspired early vampire lore.

The earliest vampires are predominantly women—perhaps as an inversion of the nurturing, life-giving ideal associated with the gender or a manifestation of early patriarchal fears of woman's "inherent" wickedness. Though vampires could target people regardless of gender or age, infants were seen as especially vulnerable. Given the high infant mortality rates present in ancient societies, this fear is understandable, as newborns were often thought of as only tenuously alive.

Garlic is also an old and widespread defense against vampires. This is one of the first plants that mankind ever cultivated agriculturally, spreading rapidly from Southeast Asia ten thousand years ago. Its apotropaic (meaning "to ward off evil") powers are attested to almost universally, and it was used to defend against demons, ghosts, and monsters in addition to vampires. Like most of the vampire defenses later devised, this herb would have been readily available for most people. Indeed, various herbs, flowers, spices, and trees have been held as vampire repellents through the ages.

The following sections describe major precursors to our modern vampire myths, from various regions across Europe and Asia.

Mesopotamian Vampires

Mesopotamia is widely considered to be the cradle of civilization. It is an umbrella term for the early societies of Babylon, Sumer, and Akkadia (to name a few of the most prominent) and is located in the present-day Middle East. The vampires of ancient Mesopotamia were demons and usually took a female form. Interestingly, many of them were thought to be created by the gods themselves, and sometimes served the interests of the gods.

The malevolent goddess Lamashtu was herself a vampiric queen of demons. Lamashtu was not worshiped by the people, but many prayers and offerings designed to ward her off have been recovered by archeologists. The goddess targeted pregnant women, unborn fetuses, and newborn infants, as she was thought to cause miscarriages and stillbirths so that she might eat the babies. She was so feared that many families would invoke other demons for protection against her.

Demons such as the *alû*, *ardate-lile*, and *lilitu* would possess the bodies of recently deceased young women in order to prey on men. Sometimes they would visit their victims while they slept, but in other cases they might masquerade as a normal woman and marry the victim outright before draining him. While these vampires could drink blood, they preferred to steal the energy and semen of their victims in order to impregnate themselves so they could eat the flesh of their children. Temples could provide families with amulets and prayers to protect their sons from this menace.

A few vampires of this period were undead humans, rather than demons. The *uruku* would rise as a ghostly revenant when someone was buried improperly, causing illness and criminal behavior in the local area. Meanwhile, the *udug* would rise from a graveyard at the behest of the gods to suck blood as a punishment when a community did not manage their graveyards properly.

Indian and Southeast Asian Vampires

Sanskrit texts from ancient India report over a dozen varieties of vampires; like their Mesopotamian counterparts, these were usually female, but some have incorporeal forms, reflecting a local preference for cremation of the dead over burial. They vary more in their origins and habits, however. The *alvantin* or *chedipe* would rise when a young woman died a sudden death, such as from childbirth; at night, they would suck blood from a victim's big toe. *Bhuta* spirits (see page 117) would rise from the grave of a person who had a physical disability and possess corpses in order to seek out fresh blood and milk. There were special shrines kept at cemeteries to placate these spirits and keep them from roaming the community, and they could be warded off by burning turmeric.

Various countries in Southeast Asia also boast vampire tales; it is possible that precursors to these in ancient Sunda (present-day Malaysia and Indonesia) were carried west through India and Mesopotamia by boat trade. In Malaysia, the *maneden* vampire inhabits the tree of the same name; it is peaceful unless humans try to harm the tree, at which point it will leap out and suck their blood. The *aswang* vampires (see page 115) of the Philippines usually drank human blood, and are difficult to catch thanks to their shapeshifting powers and their ability to create more of their kind by tricking women into consuming blood. Aswangs even train packs of crocodiles to hunt for them! These vampires are vulnerable to salt and knives, and offerings of fruit and prayers can sometimes convince them to spare a person.

Ancient Greek and Roman Vampires

The vampire lore of ancient Greece had a direct impact on the later folklore of Türkiye and Serbia (which provided the template for the modern vampire). Ancient Greeks believed that blood could be offered to call forth shades of the dead from the underworld to answer questions, as seen in the *Odyssey*. Sometimes these spirits would escape, becoming *keres* (see page 124) that stalked the battlefield, waiting to drain warriors who had fallen. However, the *empusa* (see page 127) is the clearest example of a corporeal vampire—being a beautiful woman who tempts men to her side with her charm and riches. After capturing a victim, the empusa did not drink him right away, but would fatten him up for a time to savor her meal.

In ancient Rome, the poet Ovid wrote of the *strix* (see page 135), a vampiric screech owl that would target lone travelers and unattended babies for blood. He described the way the nymph Cranae (also called Carda) used a sprig of whitethorn to repel a strix from a palace and save the young prince it had mauled. This tale was likely told to explain the existing tradition of hanging whitethorn in the doors and windows of a nursery to ward against the strix.

The avian nature of many Mediterranean vampires recalls tales of the Furies and harpies, carnivorous bird women who consumed human flesh. The *ala*, spoken of in stories across Greece and Türkiye, was a vampire in the form of an eagle who would consume sunlight as well as blood. Its approach was said to bring storms and eclipses that would starve the fields of light, destroying crops.

Jewish and Biblical Vampires

Jewish folklore dating back to ancient Mesopotamia mentions vampiric creatures, many of which were also mentioned in the Hebrew Bible. The *aluga* (literally meaning "leech") is a bloodsucking creature, variously of undead or demonic origin, mentioned in Proverbs 30:15: "The leech (greed) has two daughters, crying Give, Give. These are things that are never satisfied . . . the grave, the barren womb, the dry Earth, and the fire; these sayeth not 'It is enough.'"

The Hebrew Bible also speaks of the vampire seductresses called *lamia* (see page 129), *lilim*, or *lilitu*. These names mean "screech owl," and could be derived from the demon Lilith of Mesopotamian myth. Originally a menace to the gods and heroes of that pantheon, Lilith was reinterpreted several times in Jewish folklore. The Talmud attributed the lilitu's hunger for infants as a reflection of Lilith's sorrow that she could not bear children of her own. Ben Sira famously recast her as Adam's first wife in Eden in the eleventh century. The biblical references reflect her original function as a "night devil" (Isaiah 34:14) and "terror of the night" (Psalm 91) targeting pregnant women and children.

Several other biblical figures came to be associated with vampires, most notably Cain and Judas Iscariot. The mark of Cain, a curse from God consigning Cain to wander the Earth in punishment for spilling Abel's blood, has sometimes been interpreted as a curse of immortality, and Cain was cited as the ancestor of the monster Grendel in the Old English epic *Beowulf*. Similarly, Bulgarian vampires came to be called Children of Judas, and were thought to leave scars on their victims reading "XXX," representing the thirty pieces of silver for which Judas betrayed Jesus.

SILVER

The idea that silver could harm, or repel, vampires originated in the Slavic folklore of Eastern Europe. Silver knives and bullets were popularly attested to. One could also take a silver coin (preferably with a cross on it) and break it into shards that could be fired from a gun.

MEDIEVAL EUROPEAN VAMPIRES

The modern vampire as we know it comes from the folklore of Eastern Europe in the Middle Ages. *Vampire* (see page 136) comes from the Slavic vampyri, which may be derived from root words meaning "to drink" or "to blow." Far from the arch nobles of Gothic literature that followed them, the vampyri were animate corpses rising from paupers' graves; the fear was that any neighbor who died could become one if they were not laid to rest properly. Vampires were said to have a bloated appearance and reddish skin from gorging themselves on blood, and while they caused great destruction, they were prone to occasional comedy in folktales that suggested that (even in death) some people are doomed to foolishness.

Even though this vampire folklore developed in a region with shared linguistic and cultural components, the stories from this period are highly diverse. Vampires are sometimes incorporeal, and other times a reanimated corpse; some vampires were conflated with witches, while others were equated with werewolves. The variety of stories speaks to how local many of these oral legends were, and how intertwined vampires were with other monsters that people feared were haunting the night. Vampires could fluidly take up the role of a devil, an animalistic predator, or a wicked wizard, depending on who was telling the tale.

Strigoi

The *strigoi* was the most common subtype of vampire that appeared in Eastern European folklore in the Middle Ages. The Slavic name likely derives from the Roman strix and is likewise associated with owls. Anyone could become a strigoi after death if their soul became trapped in their body as it decomposed; this was more likely to occur if they died unhappy, or if a cat or dog passed over the body before burial.

Strigoi would usually come back to haunt their own families, at least at first. If a man died, and his relatives subsequently became ill—or livestock died on his farm, or his widow became lethargic and weak—the village might suspect he had become a strigoi and exhume his corpse. If the body was thought to be decomposing too slowly, it would be dealt with swiftly to prevent further mayhem. Methods varied between villages, but many thought that puncturing the corpse's stomach would prevent it from leaving its grave again. (The problem could even be avoided in the first place by burying the deceased with a bottle of alcohol to ease their sorrows.)

While strigoi were not always male, many stories do feature male strigoi stalking and tormenting their widows, suggesting the pattern was common in folklore. Particularly vicious strigoi might not limit their predations to their wives, even sucking the blood from their mothers, daughters, and sisters-in-law. These male vampires stand in contrast to the femme fatale type so common in ancient legends and helped expand the archetype as a whole.

OTHER EUROPEAN VAMPIRES

Another Slavic vampire was the *poroniec*, a vampire that would rise from the grave of an unbaptized infant or fetus. The high infant mortality rates of the Middle Ages meant that babies were seen as only tentatively alive at first; this made them

IDENTIFYING VAMPIRES

During the so-called "vampire craze" of the 1700s, fear of vampires was common in Eastern Europe, and sometimes the hunt for such creatures became noteworthy enough to draw the involvement of church officials, scholars, and doctors. Reports filed by these observers provide useful historical insight into how common people identified a vampire.

If a vampire was thought to be behind a village's misfortunes, locals would identify one (or several) recently deceased people who could have turned. These would then be exhumed and inspected to see if they had decomposed. At the time, people incorrectly believed that decomposition was a fast process, so any corpse that hadn't become a skeleton in a short time span might be suspect. These "vampires" had flushed skin, a lot of blood remaining in the body, long hair and nails, swollen stomachs, and marks about the neck—all normal stages of the decomposition process! Once a corpse was identified as a vampire, it was usually destroyed in some fashion to end the threat it posed.

Some of these surviving records also mention superstitions about vampires. In some places, people thought the blood of a vampire could be used to cure victims they had sickened; in one instance where this was attempted, however, the decaying corpse's blood killed the recipient. It was also believed that any livestock killed by a vampire should be burned, and not consumed, as one would otherwise become a vampire as well.

especially vulnerable to perversions of the line between life and death. These vampire babies would haunt their mothers, but could be appeased through magical rituals that transformed them into spiritual protectors of their living families.

Greece had its own fascinating vampire lore during this time. Children born between Christmas and New Year's (what was called "the unclean days" in Bulgaria and Moldova due to the lack of Christian rituals performed during this time of rest for the priests) were thought destined to be vampires, even including those born on Christmas! Though it seems ironic, the belief was that mothers would be punished for hubris for birthing a child on the same day as the Virgin Mary. In the right circumstances, however, anyone could become a vampire; most commonly, those who lived sinful lives or whose relatives neglected them in death would rise up from their graves. Unlike their Slavic counterparts, however, Greek vampires were usually more pitied than feared, as they were often described merely as miserable souls wandering the Earth in the clutches of the devil. However, in some cases the vampire would return to its home and attack the living, "suffocating" them to death by stealing their breath and blood through the nose. Such tales were used to reinforce the importance of proper funeral rites, which involved extensive cleansing of the body and honoring the spirit.

THE PLAGUE OF VAMPIRES

In Europe, vampires came to be closely associated with plagues and outbreaks of disease, especially the bubonic plague. Plague season would begin in the summer and last through the warm weather of autumn, as it was spread by fleas. During that time of year, people died so rapidly that many bodies were buried in shallow mass graves without any funeral rites. However, bodies in shallow graves decompose faster, especially when it's warm out. Such graves may swell or sink as the corpse releases gases (which can even cause a faint glow above graves at night if atmospheric conditions are right). Dogs and other animals might dig up these graves seeking food, exposing hands and feet above the soil. It's no wonder that people came to believe that those who died of plague were more likely to become vampires, as any of these sights might seem like a sign of undead activity!

People not only believed that plagues created vampires, but also that vampires could bring plagues to a community. A sudden outbreak of disease was often seen as a sign of vampiric activity, as was the case in Transylvania in 1709. Locals there believed the devil had set vampires on the town to destroy them, which led them to dig up four bodies (including a priest!) and stake them. Similar activities were documented in Greece, Poland, and Hungary, suggesting that vampire hunts were a widespread response to epidemics. While such hunts could not provide any real relief, perhaps they helped residents feel some sense of control during a time when people did not understand how illnesses spread.

Diseases Associated with Vampirism

Some historical records describing vampires include details that have led researchers to speculate that undiagnosed diseases may have been behind some cases of vampirism.

Porphyria: In the 1980s, biochemist David Dolphin proposed that medieval "vampires" may have had porphyria, a disorder that can cause blotchy red skin, seizures, hallucinations, stomach pain, and bloody urine. Porphyria patients can also develop a severe sunlight sensitivity, leading them to avoid daytime outings. Dolphin's theory was based on the idea that people in the Middle Ages tried to treat porphyria by drinking cow's blood, though this was later debunked.

Rabies: Although cases are now rare in the United States, the disease was striking fear into people's hearts as recently as the 1920s. The rabies virus originates in bats and is transmitted through bites, whereupon it begins a slow crawl up the nerves to the brain. By the time symptoms begin, rabies is fatal, even with today's modern medicine. Those affected develop a fever, agitation, confusion, and an extreme fear of water. Since the virus spreads through bites, it induces violent behavior in the host to create such opportunities. Given how endemic rabies is across the world, it is easy to imagine that a bad outbreak would be explained in terms of vampirism.

Cholera: European imperialism in the nineteenth century led to bacterial cholera making its way west from Asia. Outbreaks in England and Ireland were severe, in part because people did not realize the infection was spread through contaminated water and were only taking precautions against airborne contagion. During successive waves of the epidemic (starting in 1826 and ending in 1896), medical knowledge had advanced enough that people were less likely to believe that vampires actually caused cholera (or vice versa), but the two were linked in the public imagination nonetheless. Poets described cholera

as a vampire haunting London, and when cremation was legalized in 1885 to help combat the disease, journalists were quick to compare the situation to the old-fashioned methods of disposal of "vampire" corpses.

ROMANTICISM AND LITERATURE

Our modern conception of vampires is largely rooted in the literary depictions of the nineteenth century. Prior to that point, vampires had existed mainly within the realm of oral folklore. As news of vampire hunts in Eastern Europe made their way west into France and England, vampires captured the public imagination in a new way.

Vampires began appearing in the work of notable English poets such as Samuel Taylor Coleridge and John Keats in the early nineteenth century, which provided inspiration to

fellow writers Lord Byron and John William Polidori. Byron and Polidori were friends with Mary Shelley, the creator of *Frankenstein*, and they would often go on writing trips together to work on poems and novels. After discussing vampires on one such occasion in 1819, Polidori wrote the short story "The Vampyre," widely considered the vampire's official debut in English literature. Incorporating elements of the Gothic and Romantic genres, the story was an instant hit; its antagonist, the mysterious vampire Lord Ruthven, could be considered a prototype of Count Dracula.

Over the next few decades, "The Vampyre" enjoyed a number of stage adaptations across Europe, and vampire novels began appearing more often. In 1872, Irish writer Joseph Sheridan Le Fanu published *Carmilla*, a novella about a female vampire seducing and preying on innocent maidens. Historical records show that Bram Stoker read and enjoyed *Carmilla* prior to writing *Dracula*. He spent several years doing careful research about vampire folklore (using the patchy sources available in English at the time) before publishing *Dracula* in 1897. The same year, Florence Marryat published *The Blood of the Vampire*, which initially sold much better than *Dracula* due to the writer's higher profile.

Ironically, these English-speaking writers were unaware of another important vampire story published in 1880. The Serbian novel *After Ninety Years*, by Milovan Glišić, adapted a popular folktale about the vampire Sava Savanović (see page 142) and incorporates a great deal of fascinating information about the vampire beliefs of that time. However, Glišić's novel was not translated into English until 2015, so even though it would likely have been of interest to writers like Bram Stoker, it did not have any influence on the vampires of English literature.

MODERN REVIVAL

Vampires became a staple of film and television when these technologies arrived in the twentieth century. Characters like Dracula and Carmilla, alongside fictionalized versions of historical figures like Elizabeth Báthory (see page 94), increasingly appeared in films in the United States and the United Kingdom in the 1960s and '70s. However, vampires were largely relegated to the horror genre during this time.

Things began to change thanks to two very different vampire stories. The Gothic soap opera *Dark Shadows* premiered in 1966, featuring a unique cast of characters such as werewolves, witches, and ghosts. The vampire character Barnabas Collins was the most popular, owing in part to the romantic tragedy in his past that often motivated him to pursue ill-fated plots to seduce women. In 1976, Anne Rice published *Interview with the Vampire* (see page 154), the first book of her long-running series The Vampire Chronicles. Rice's book was controversial upon its release, but soon came to be enormously popular and influential. *Dark Shadows* and *Interview with the Vampire* helped bring vampires out of the horror genre by turning them into tragic, romantic figures marked by loneliness. They also helped associate vampires with specific areas of the United States, such as New England and New Orleans.

As the goth and punk scenes developed in the 1980s, vampire fiction saw new opportunities for transformation. Game designer Mark Rein-Hagen was inspired to create a new vampire game during a road trip through the Midwest, where he imagined vampires haunting the many abandoned warehouses and factories he saw in towns impacted by industrial decline. *Vampire: The Masquerade* (see page 157) debuted in 1991, surprising a tabletop gaming market dominated by fantasy titles like *Dungeons & Dragons*. The game became a hit with fans of goth and punk culture, spawning a live-action role-play version called *Mind's Eye Theatre* that became a staple at many music clubs and conventions. The vampire fascination spurred on by the game has been credited with inspiring later works like *Underworld* and *True Blood* (The Southern Vampire Mysteries, see page 166).

Core and Abilities

Since vampires usually appear more or less human, it is fair to say that they are mainly distinguished by their specific abilities and weaknesses. Most of us are probably envisioning a pale, strong individual, with senses and strength well beyond any mortal, yet driven back by simple sunlight and garlic. These classic characteristics help us distinguish between vampires and, say, werewolves or fairies.

Yet the scope and variation of vampiric powers in folklore extends well beyond what you might see in modern movies today. Vampires might shapeshift into unexpected forms (such as a goose), walk unhindered in daylight, or be weak to even an ordinary glass bottle, depending on who was telling the story. This chapter explores the most common characteristics vampires share, exploring their origins and peculiarities.

THE BASICS

Vampire stories around the world include an incredible variety
of elements, many of which never made it into the standard
depiction of vampires in Western popular culture. In this
chapter, I will discuss some of the common themes of vampire
folklore, and the most common abilities (and weaknesses)
of vampires. Some of the topics covered here are very old,
stretching back to the earliest myths, while others are fairly
recent inventions. I hope you will find this breakdown useful
for gaining a deeper understanding of what makes vampires
unique among the monsters of human imagination.

Immortality

In ancient mythology, immortality is usually the exclusive
province of gods and demons. For example, the ancient Greeks
believed that the only way for a human to gain immortality was
to be resurrected by the gods, or to be born from the union of
god and human. Beyond that, the immortality of many other
creatures in Greek myth is usually inferred; while many monsters

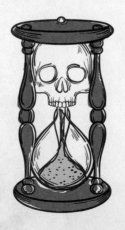

were stated to be impervious to mortal attacks, it wasn't always clear whether they could age or die of other causes.

Traditional vampire folklore is similar in this respect. Since most vampires were thought to be undead or demons, they were seen as having strength greater than a human, and they could survive indefinitely on the vitality of the living. Some tales from Eastern Europe did explicitly use the word *immortal*, though usually this power was attributed to only one part of the vampire. For example, a Romani eyewitness describing a vampire hunt to an anthropologist in 1949 stated, "If the body is dead and the soul has escaped, some part must remain alive, for some part of the human lives forever and is immortal." This is reminiscent of how the *vetala*, an Indian vampiric spirit created by the improper death rites given to a child, could possess any corpse and was immortal only in the sense that the soul could move on to another body if its current host was destroyed. Limiting the vampire's immortality in this way left open the possibility that they could still be killed.

Bloodsuckers

Blood-drinking is one of the most common traits seen in vampire stories around the world. Thousands of years ago, our ancient ancestors already knew that blood was necessary for life and believed that vampiric creatures would feast on human blood (see "Vampire History," page 29). While it is unclear whether dead bodies were dug up during vampire hunts in ancient times, anyone doing so would have observed the same blood pooling on the lips and mouth of decomposing corpses that later inspired fear in the hearts of medieval Europeans.

So, it is likely that the idea of the dead drinking human blood was originally an attempt to interpret the unnerving state of dead bodies.

The blood-drinking of vampires may also be a metaphor for death itself. In medieval Greece, Orthodox Christian tradition required many elaborate funeral preparations for the body; some of these were explained as ways to prevent the deceased from becoming a vampire, while others were meant to ward off the influence of Charos (Death) after he had claimed that person's soul. Charos was thought to invisibly cut the throat of his victims with a blade (in the same way humans slaughter livestock), resulting in spiritual "blood" splashing the home and any nearby family. While this was not literal blood, it necessitated washing the area carefully just the same. Thus, blood-spilling is the natural province of death, as a way to release the soul from the body. Conversely, when a soul does not leave a corpse after death, it becomes a vampire, who then unnaturally drinks the blood of the living.

The Undead

Undeath is another classical vampire attribute that existed long before Dracula. Most of the folklore sees the vampire as a specific individual who dies, and then returns (either in body or spirit) as a predatory monster. This is readily apparent in the novel *After Ninety Years*, a retelling of a traditional Serbian story, when a town plagued by a vampire must first find out his name, and then find its unmarked, ninety-year-old grave in order to destroy it. This type of vampire is the standard in Europe, and many vampires in the Middle East and South Asia are similar.

WHY BLOOD?

The idea that vampires drink blood is probably the single most common fact people know about them today. However, this is not true for all vampire myths. Most vampires consume the vitality or life of the living, which takes various forms.

Some vampires preferred to steal human breath for their nourishment, resulting in death by suffocation. This is the case with several kinds of Scandinavian *draugrs* (see page 121) and Japanese creatures such as the *nobusuma*, a bat that becomes a vampire if it lives long enough.

Others would consume human energy in the form of emotions. The Danish *gienganger* (see page 122) feeds on fear by haunting a home, while the Ukrainian *mavka* prefers to consume human joy by tickling its victims—to death! However, the most common energy vampires by far are the femme fatale types (such as the lilitu, see page 131) who seduce humans and steal away their life force through sexual acts.

Some vampire tales describe them eating organs, usually the liver or intestines. While this is very uncommon in our modern vampire fiction, it is another piece of vampire lore that probably has its roots in observable phenomena. When scavenging predators dig up bodies seeking food, they usually prefer to start with the liver before consuming other soft organs (such as the intestines). When daylight came and locals saw the grisly remains, they could easily have blamed it on vampires feasting on the dead.

However, some vampires that are undead arise from places of death, rather than being a specific person. They usually use cemeteries or execution sites as their home base, possessing whatever corpses are intact to target those who pass by. Vampire-like creatures such as the Arabic *ghoul* and *algul*, and the Indian *pacu pati* and *pisacha*, are examples of this type of undead creature that more closely resembles what we would call a zombie in modern times. Other vampiric spirits would take a ghostly or skeletal appearance, such as the mysterious Washer Woman of the Night. Old stories in England and France describe her appearing after sunset, weeping and washing the burial shrouds of unbaptized babies in the river. If anyone sees her, she makes them join her in washing until sunrise; anyone who declines, or doesn't perform the task to her standards, is killed. Stories like these demonstrate that early vampires had a lot in common with ghosts and other types of undead spirits, rather than always being physically corporeal.

ABILITIES

The vampire's powers make them a powerful adversary that any ordinary human would struggle to escape from (or vanquish). In films, we see vampires that are strong and beautiful, able to fly, hypnotize people, change forms, and recover from any nonlethal wounds. These powers, and more, have their roots in the vampire lore of our ancestors. Yet there are other powers attributed to vampires that are largely forgotten now, like their ability to send their soul flying out of their body in the form of a butterfly. As the literary vampires of John William Polidori, Bram Stoker, and others took hold of popular culture, our conception of what vampires could do became narrower over time.

In this section you will find information about the abilities attributed to the vampires of old, as well as some that are newer additions to the lore. It is important to keep in mind that most vampire stories do not include all of these elements, instead featuring a selection of them based on the culture and trends of the time. Indeed, any vampire endowed with all of these gifts would be a fearsome thing!

Regeneration

In most modern fiction, vampires seem to be able to recover from any wounds that don't kill them, often at a remarkably fast pace. By comparison, the traditional vampires were usually invulnerable to many kinds of attacks (such as bladed weapons) but could not necessarily repair damage to their physical bodies. Slavic vampire tales, and records of actual vampire hunts, often mentioned that when a vampire was found in their coffin, they would often still show the wounds that townsfolk defending themselves had inflicted the night before. Even more curious, in Serbian stories where the vampire could vacate their current body and seek out a new host, the new body might then manifest whatever wounds the previous one had at the time of transfer.

The ability to regenerate the body seems to have originally been more common to demonic, rather than undead, vampires. Hindu myths recount the demon Ravana, king of the blood-drinking *rakshasas* (see page 131), as being able to instantly heal from any wound (including a lost limb)! The Egyptian goddess Sekhmet shares this trait with Ravana. Not only was she the goddess of vampires, but it was also believed in ancient Egypt that she would share her healing secrets with her most devout priests (though they might have to face a vampire to first show their worthiness).

Most of the time, vampires healed just like you or me, by resting up and consuming plenty of food. A vampire who was injured was likely to seek out more prey to replenish their strength, so keeping them away from people was imperative if you were hunting one. A few rare vampires would have to consume something other than blood to heal, like the *estrie*—an incorporeal femme fatale vampire of medieval Europe—who could only recover from her wounds if she ate the bread and salt of the human who injured her.

Flight

Flight was a fairly common feature in vampire tales, though this was often facilitated by shapeshifting into a flying animal (such as a bat, owl, or butterfly; see page 66). It was less common for vampires to fly while in human form, but not unheard of. Filipino aswangs could usually fly, as could some *jiangshi* (see page 123) from the myths of North China and Mongolia. A few European vampires, such as the *alp* of Germany, could also fly, owing to their demonic powers. One very unusual example is the *impundulu* of South Africa, a small red vampire only 3 inches (8 cm) tall that pilots a flying machine powered by blood! Ironically, while the impundulu looks like a bird, it cannot fly on its own. Meanwhile, the Indigenous Iroquois people of what is now known as New York told tales of vampires called flying heads that would flap their hair in the air as they soared through the night. Though these vampires were exceedingly fast and nimble, they were easily deceived, and so people would lure them close to their campfires before trapping and burning them.

Overall, flying vampires are most common in stories from Southeast Asia, the Pacific Islands, and the Americas. Since immigration and trade routes over sea and land existed between these regions in ancient times, modern researchers attribute folklore similarities such as these to shared origins thousands of years ago.

Mind Control

Many modern vampire stories describe vampires as being able to hypnotize people to obey their commands or put them in a kind of trance that keeps them docile while they are killed; you may have seen this on *Buffy the Vampire Slayer*, *True Blood*, *The Vampire Diaries* (see page 165), or any number of other TV shows. Strictly speaking, this ability is a more modern element of vampire fiction, although there are precedents for it in the traditional folklore.

The idea that vampires could use hypnosis was first introduced in the vampire fiction of the nineteenth century. Carmilla approached her victims at night, and they remembered her only as a strange dream. Likewise, Dracula influenced Mina Harker's mind and caused her to sleepwalk, though she was later hypnotized by the hunter Van Helsing to counter this. Europe was enjoying a fascination with hypnotism at the time when these books were written, so it makes sense that these novels would have incorporated it as a way to make their vampires even more alluring and dangerous.

In older vampire stories, mind control is not a common vampiric trait, but exceptions exist. The Croatian *pijavica* could read minds as well as plant suggestions, but since they always targeted their own family members, it's unclear whether they could use these powers on just anyone. Usually, vampires with the ability to influence the mind did so using magic. In Portugal, for example, the *bruja* (meaning "witch") was not just a spellcaster but also an inhuman spirit with vampiric abilities. They could read minds, hypnotize people, and even see the future, yet these abilities were mainly used in service of finding their next meal of blood.

Strength

The strength of a vampire is a curious double-edged sword. Eyewitnesses interviewed during vampire hunts in the nineteenth century agreed that the undead were powerful at night, but nearly harmless during the day. The Serbian writer Joakim Vujić once asked a monk in Kosovo how it was that the people of Novi Pazar village could stake a vampire in its coffin, when the vampire could have fought back. The monk replied, "What nonsense is this? How could he grab hold of us, when during the day he is dead and has no strength; only at night does he regain strength from the devil, and come to life to terrorize the village." Clearly, Eastern Europeans at the time thought of vampires as fluctuating in strength from day to night.

Of course, after darkness fell, a vampire quickly gained strength greater than any human. Today, we usually imagine vampires as chasing down humans as prey, overwhelming us with force in order to land a bite. But eighteenth- and nineteenth-century vampire stories are even more grisly than this; in Germany, Norway, and Bosnia, vampires were said to pick up entire cows and crush them to death, just to better squeeze the blood out! Vampires might also use their strength to drop enormous boulders on people, or even cause avalanches or mudslides if they were backed into a corner.

It's interesting that female vampires were usually described as equally as strong as their male counterparts, though they were less likely to show it. Usually, people expected that men could be willingly lured in by a female vampire's beauty, so she would have less need to resort to violence. The reverse could sometimes be true as well; in Transylvania, young women were warned of a handsome male vampire called a *zemu* who also preferred to use seduction rather than strength.

Heightened Senses

Vampires were usually thought to have very sharp senses, especially vision and hearing. In Romania and Serbia, it was unlucky to even say the words "vampire," "revenant," "werewolf," and the like, since these creatures were believed to be able to hear their names spoken at any distance. Vampires could, of course, see in the dark, though in some cases their vision could still be fooled by shadows and other tricks of the light.

There is also the animalistic quality of each vampire variant to consider. Many of them can shapeshift into prolific hunters, especially owls and wolves. An owl's keen night vision and the incomparable hearing and sense of smell that a wolf possesses can translate to these heightened senses as well. Additionally, many Balkan vampires, such as the *vrykolaka*, have a foggy line

MAGIC

While being a vampire was no guarantee of magical abilities, some vampires were also talented witches or sorcerers. This not only made them more powerful predators but also endowed them with sage wisdom that humans would occasionally be brave enough to seek out!

between vampires and werewolves, which are well known for their wolf-sharp senses.

Finally, a Chinese vampire, the jiangshi (see page 123), is known for being particularly good at scenting their prey and tracking them down. This could be true for other vampires when their folklore trends to being more animalistic in nature. When vampires see humans as prey, it seems only logical that they would have the instincts and sensory faculties of a predator.

Shapeshifter

The ability to transform into animals and other forms is common in the vampire stories of many regions. In *Dracula*, the vampire transforms into a wolf, a dog, a bat, and even a thin vapor that could penetrate the smallest cracks. These animal forms come directly from German folklore, where vampires could additionally take the form of rats and snakes. Yugoslavia also spoke of vampires taking the shape of a snake, owing to the latter's reputation for immortality (via shedding its skin). In Chile, the aquatic *cai cai vilu* vampire was said to take on the form of oxen, horses, or an ocean wave; eagle and owl forms were common in Bavaria and Türkiye. In Indonesia, vampires could become tigers, while the Philippines said they could turn into alligators.

You may notice that most of these animals are predators in their own right, which might plausibly attack a human on occasion. But forms like a pig, cat, rat, spider, or flea would help a vampire go incognito and stalk its prey while avoiding detection, making them dangerous as well. The Greek vampires that could turn into fire or water may have been an inspiration for Dracula's vapor form (since the South American examples would not have been known in England at the time). Vampires who were also sorcerers or witches could sometimes disguise themselves as specific humans as well, making them very effective at luring and ambushing their victims.

Invisibility

The ability to become invisible is another classic vampire attribute found all over the world. In some cases, the vampire had true invisibility, while in other cases the vampire would simply shapeshift into air or shrink to such a small size that they were nearly impossible to spot. Regardless, the overall effect was the same. In Europe, invisibility was most common in the vampire stories of Germany and Bulgaria, but it was even more widespread in Arab cultures and in India. One can also find invisible vampires in Mongolia, across the Pacific Islands, and in the Indigenous cultures of Australia.

Since vampires often became invisible by changing into a gas or vapor, one might expect that they would be invulnerable to attack at the same time. However, this method left vampires open to a particular type of trap. A vampire hunter could take a strong bottle, add a drop of blood to it, and leave it out at night someplace where a vampire could find it. When the vampire slipped into the bottle to have a snack, a vampire hunter would quickly seal the bottle with a waxed cork that had the image of a saint pressed into it. This sanctified seal would trap the vampire until such time that the bottle could be thrown into a fire to roast until it cracked and exploded, killing the vampire! The one downside to this plan is that it required the hunter to be able to see the vampire while they were invisible, or else they would not know when to seal the bottle. However, Bulgarians believed that a *dhampir* (see page 120), the mortal child of a vampire and a human, could accomplish this.

Astral Projection

For many vampires, the soul and the body were not irrevocably bound together. Some could separate the soul for periods of time to roam as a spirit; this was especially true of vampiric spirits who would merely possess a corpse for convenience in the same way a crab can move from shell to shell. In some cultures it was feared that witches could become living vampires, who could astral project to drink life energy at night while appearing to simply sleep in bed.

In the Slavic folktales of Eastern Europe, a vampire's soul could escape their body in the form of a butterfly or moth. If a vampire had been tracked back to their coffin, it was critical that anyone preparing to stake them had at least one assistant to pour holy water down the vampire's throat. Otherwise, a butterfly might emerge from its mouth, allowing the soul to flee while the body was destroyed. Panicked locals would therefore chase down and burn any butterflies or moths seen nearby

during a vampire hunt. The Serbian film *Leptirica* (1973, see page 143) shows the soul of the vampire Sava Savanović escaping destruction in this way, only to possess a local woman to continue his reign of terror. While most of us probably don't associate butterflies with evil, the superstition that they are vampiric spirits has persisted into the modern day in some rural parts of Europe.

Speed

As a predator that hunts humans, vampires benefit from being supernaturally fast. Writings from ancient Mesopotamia in the Middle East warned of the lilitu moving faster than the eye could see, and this type of description continued to appear in stories from around the Mediterranean well into the nineteenth century. Arabic, Greek, and Angolan stories characterized vampires as not only fast but also incredibly agile, moving with the grace and precision of cats. Their speed may have also been somewhat metaphorical; since plagues were believed to be caused by vampires, it would make sense to think that a vampire could cover a lot of ground very quickly, just as contagions rapidly spread from village to village.

Some vampires were especially fast, like the Serbian *veshtitza*, but at the cost of physical strength and durability. But others, like the German *dodelecker*, were too slow and clumsy to catch anyone! In contrast to the many German vampires who were both strong and fast, the dodelecker struggled even to exit its coffin, and would stumble and crawl about night after night crying out for someone to come feed it. People could easily outrun it, and after a few years it would starve to death and haunt the graveyard no more.

Preternatural Beauty

Traditional vampire lore diverges greatly on the appearance of vampires. Some are utterly gorgeous, taking advantage of their appearance to seduce (and even marry) young people to slowly consume their vitality. Many female vampires were like this, though there were male vampires who used the same tactics as well. But this attribute was mainly impressive because the average vampire was a hideous, decomposing creature. The appearance of corpses dug up during medieval European vampire hunts informed legends of vampires that were bloated and twisted, with open wounds, reddened skin, long nails, and blood pouring from their mouth and eyes. These rotting vampires were unlikely to ever be mistaken for the living, let alone offered a marriage proposal.

Those vampires that were blessed with supernatural beauty were so irresistible that their charm was thought to have magical origins. In such cases, spells or amulets could be used

BUTTERFLIES

Why would butterflies, of all things, be associated so strongly with vampires? Butterflies are attracted to a gaseous chemical called trimethylene, which is given off by dead bodies. They can often be seen clustering over fresh graves, or even sipping on spilt blood! The hawthorn tree, thought to kill vampires, also gives off trimethylene.

to try to break the vampire's influence over their human thralls. In ancient Carthage (a city in present-day Tunisia) a man seduced by the vampire goddess Aisha Qandisha could send her away by plunging an iron knife into the ground. Once her spell was broken, he would be able to see that she had the legs and hooves of a goat. Iron objects, known for their protective powers, were also used to protect against the influence of vampires in medieval Europe. Iron needles pinned to clothes, nails in doorframes, and scissors under beds were used to ensure that humans would not be tricked by the enchanting beauty of vampires that might approach them.

WEAKNESSES

Around the world, countless methods for preventing, warding off, or harming vampires exist, each tailored to the weaknesses of the local variants. Some vampire weaknesses are quite well known, having been standardized and brought into the mainstream by *Dracula* and other works of fiction. Unfortunately, the same trends that popularized vampires accelerated the process of forgetting the traditional lore, some of which is lost forever. In Germany, for example, records mention a song that could be sung by the fireplace by the last person to go to bed at night, which would prevent any vampires from entering the home until sunrise. The lyrics and melody have faded into obscurity.

In this section I review the most important common vampire weaknesses and explain their origins. While many of the protective measures found in vampire lore are no longer practiced, some of them remain alive and well in traditional communities. Some people may look down on these superstitions, but they are a valuable reminder of how the fear of vampires has followed mankind through history.

Sunlight

Most vampires were active only at night, as their powers were much stronger after the sun had set. In places like Romania and Serbia, vampires were completely immobile and dead during the day. For this reason, most ordinary folk would only hunt them during the day, when the odds were more in their favor.

It should be noted that not all vampires in folklore were actually harmed by sunlight (despite the fact that this has become a nearly universal trend in modern vampire fiction). In stories where vampires were that weak to sunlight, the biggest challenge was getting them into a situation where they might actually be exposed to it. One curious method was to present the vampire with some puzzle or challenge to keep them occupied until the sun rose. Vampires might get distracted trying to undo a tangled knot or be compelled to pick up spilled grains on the ground, and then fail to escape in time. While this might make vampires seem very unintelligent, this sort of trick could be found in traditional stories about many different supernatural creatures, including witches, fairies, werewolves, and more.

Silver

Accounts varied as to what sort of weapon was best for battling a vampire. Often the issue came down to what material was used to craft the weapon (or its ammunition). A variety of metals were cited as effective against vampires, including gold, silver, lead, steel, and iron. Each of these metals has a unique body of lore describing its mystical properties, both in oral folklore and in esoteric practices like alchemy. Iron, for example, has long been held to offer protection against curses and spells, fairies, and other supernatural creatures. Gold and silver were often associated with the sun and moon, respectively, which may explain why they were thought to have some influence over vampiric creatures.

The vampire folktales of Eastern Europe often called for a combination of metals to be used in slaying a vampire; one account said that gold, silver, and lead should all be melted together to form bullets that would be shot into the vampire's coffin. In other cases, silver alone might suffice, but it would need to be blessed by a priest or coated beforehand in holy water or the vampire's own blood. Silver from coins that had religious

symbols stamped on them was also valued, as it could be melted down or broken into pieces that could be fired from a gun.

Later, silver became the standard metal of choice against vampires, once again due to Bram Stoker's influence. He played up the sacred power of silver to repel vampires in *Dracula* after reading that it was used in vampire hunts. Subsequent writers adopted this trope and exaggerated it further, until stories like *True Blood* (The Southern Vampire Mysteries, see page 166) depicted silver literally burning vampires on contact!

Running Water

Although the idea that vampires cannot cross running water is now popular in Western vampire fiction, it may have first appeared in China. The jiangshi (see page 123) was thought to have great difficulty crossing running water, perhaps because it had poor eyesight and very stiff joints. Conversely, some European vampires (such as the lamia, or the Washerwoman of the Night) had a special affinity for water and preferred to hunt near streams and rivers. The Scottish nuckelavee was a rare example of a European vampire that could not cross running water, as this vampiric fey was bound to a particular body of fresh water such as a lake or pond.

The idea that vampires cannot cross running water may be another reflection of the connection between vampires and plagues. Drinking water from stagnant sources, such as ponds, increases the chances of contamination from bacteria and other disease vectors. Even prior to the scientific discovery of disease-causing microorganisms, people understood this and obtained water from moving sources like rivers and streams whenever possible. Eventually, people may have started to see this clean, running water as not just being free of disease but also having the power to repel disease, and the undead who were thought to cause it. Eventually, Western vampire stories came to incorporate the running water weakness more often. It was then explained as a reference to Jesus's baptism in the Jordan River.

Consent

Many fictional vampires require permission from a resident to enter a home. Consent from the vampire's victim can be given under duress or as a result of psychic compulsion from the intruding vampire. Modern folklorists also interpret consent in other ways; for example, having a doormat that says "Welcome" can be considered an invitation to enter for vampires. A popular thought experiment also begs the question if a vampire cop would be able to gain entry to a home with a warrant from a judge, and the debate that comes from this dialectical exercise is born out of what exactly "permission for entry" means.

For the purposes of this book, we'll be considering consent as what a vampire needs to enter someone's house. The folkloric roots of consent are a little muddied, but it may derive from a few different factors. One origin could be that the myriad ways of repelling a vampire—garlic, running water, thorny bramble—are the antitheses of consent. Therefore, a vampire would have to have a willing victim (or at the very least, someone ignorant of the vampiric threat) to allow them entry into a home. Vampires in folklore also often visit their families and request peculiar objects (their shoes or a meal have been historically cited) and can get perturbed when their requests are denied.

Additionally, undead revenant vampires with spirits freshly returned to their dead bodies might abide by spirit rules. There are many cultures that speak of ways to invite spirits into your home—especially those that are floating on Earth in the forty days it takes them to find their way to the afterlife. As previously mentioned, leaving windows open was as good as an invitation for spirits of the dead to enter your home before they passed on to another plane.

For vampires that are more demonic than human, consenting to your torment is something that Christian devils and demons love to coax out of their victims. It is less of a hindrance for demons, and more of a challenge. That is where the true power of devils and demons comes from, after all; it isn't in the torment they wreak but the part they make people play in it.

Garlic and Herbs

Perhaps due to its antibacterial qualities (which can help prevent infections), garlic has been viewed as a protective herb in many countries for thousands of years. It is traditionally a major weakness of vampires in Europe, the Middle East, Africa, and Asia. This highly versatile bulb could be hung over

MAY I COME IN?

The origin of this superstition comes from some European cultures (Hungarian and Serbian, in particular, with accounts in Ireland, Denmark, and Poland) believing that leaving the window open for the spirits of the recently deceased would show them respect and help them move on to the afterlife. Shutting the window revokes the spirit's ability and this disrespect could result in a malevolent spirit.

windows and doors, infused into oil and rubbed on the body, added to bathwater or mop buckets, or even ingested to "fill the blood" with its scent or make the blood bitter to taste. In Romania, Saint Andrew's Day was a traditional time for employing all these methods to ensure that vampires could not come near one's family, home, or livestock.

Other plants have also been used to defend against vampires. Flowering plants such as poisonous aconite or whitethorn were hung in windows, while the thorny shrubs like blackthorn, dogrose, or jeruju provided branches for people to lay over graves to snag and stab vampires. Spices like turmeric could be burned as incense to drive away vampires or keep them confined to a cemetery. Before the modern era, people had detailed knowledge of local plants and maintained detailed oral folklore about their special powers, leading to many different plants being linked to vampire lore in some way. Unfortunately, many early written sources about vampire folklore are vague

SHROUDS

If you've ever seen a Dracula costume on Halloween, you know that the cape is a key component. The dark cloak associated with vampires was originally a white burial shroud. Vampires rising from their graves were said to continue wearing the shroud, and in some cases it offered magical protection!

on this point, alluding to "magical herbs" used to craft arrows, salves, and wards but are not always named. Those seeking information on plants used against vampires in a given region can start by looking at which plants were seen as protective generally, and then investigating those linked to the dead.

OBJECTS OF POWER

While vampires possess numerous powers and abilities on their own, some also wield powerful magic tools that further augment their capabilities. In some cases these objects were things the vampire had been buried with, or possessed while still alive, but often they were made by vampires who were talented sorcerers. This meant that some of the same remedies attributed to witches (such as ointments or potions of youth) would show up in vampire stories as well.

Some vampires, like the Irish fey *leanan sidhe*, possessed magical tools that would grow stronger as they fed on more victims. The leanan sidhe would add a little blood from each man she preyed on to her cauldron, which would gradually make her stronger as its powers grew. Other vampires had items that could let them fly, turn invisible, or protect themselves from attacks. This meant that vampire hunters would often have to find ways to disarm their foes or destroy these items, in order to fight their quarry on more even ground.

Hoard

Even before modern people began to imagine vampires as ancient aristocrats in castles, some were already covetously guarding hoards of treasure. This might seem surprising if you grew up on stories like *The Hobbit*, in which dragons are the ones that guard caves full of gold. But the idea of vampires defending treasure makes more sense when we realize that they are defending the riches they were buried with, in their own tombs!

While many common folks were simply buried in shrouds or coffins, there have always been more elaborate methods of burial for those of higher status or wealth. In ancient times, kings, generals, priests, and others would often have elaborate tombs constructed, which were filled with valuable items for the deceased to take with them into the afterlife. It was inevitable that these would become tempting targets for thieves, but sometimes those who dared tread on sacred ground would return claiming to have been chased off by the deceased, who was now a vampire unwilling to part with his property! The Scandinavian draugr fits this template well, as does the corpse candle, a vampiric spirit from Germany and Switzerland that manifests as a light over its grave.

In other cases, a vampire might be made or recruited by a living witch or sorcerer to guard their treasures. The *biloko* of Congolese folklore, which uses a magical bell to put intruders to sleep before eating them, is one example.

Familiars

The concept of vampire familiars has changed dramatically over time. Thanks once again to Bram Stoker's *Dracula*, many modern vampire stories include humans who willingly serve a vampire in the hopes of eventually being granted immortality themselves. These relationships are often dangerous and abusive, though the television show *What We Do in the Shadows* (2019) has also parodied the concept. However, traditional vampire stories rarely include humans in this role.

Some vampires, especially those who were witches or sorcerers, would keep animal familiars. Frequently the animal was one the vampire could also transform into, suggesting that the shapeshifting ability granted the vampire the loyalty of that species. In the Philippines, the vampire aswang could command large numbers of alligators, while the Russian *upiór* would use innocuous familiars like insects or chickens to scope out farms before creeping in to eat livestock and children.

However, the most common familiars found in vampire folklore are the vampires themselves! Many vampiric spirits were coveted as familiars by nefarious spellcasters, although securing the loyalty of an independent vampire was difficult. In many cases it was easier to simply make a vampire yourself, which would follow your commands. In Poland, for example, many people feared that witches would curse expectant mothers to miscarry, so that they could dig up the unbaptized fetus and transform it into a vampiric spirit called a poroniec. These vampire babies could wreak havoc if they were sent to target their grieving families, so some areas had special funeral customs for stillbirths to prevent this.

Coffin

Most modern vampire stories treat a vampire's coffin as a comfortable bed they return to each day, which protects them from the sun's rays and any prying eyes. Vampires caught without a coffin might struggle to make do by digging underground or concealing themselves in an enclosed space (such as the covered bathtub used by the young vampire Eli in the film *Let the Right One In*). While traditional vampire lore treats coffins in much the same way, these boxes are sometimes more of a weakness for the vampire than an asset.

In places where people had the time and money to bury the dead in coffins, they would sometimes try to construct them in a vampire-proof way. Coffins could be lined with sacred herbs or rows of spiky thorns to stab any corpse that started moving on its own. The deceased could be set in the coffin upside down (so that any attempt to escape would only lead them to dig deeper) or nailed into the wood by the feet. In the most extreme cases, where the community felt with certainty that a wicked person was sure to become a vampire, a sarcophagus would be constructed out of stone, and hot lead poured over the corpse before burial!

During repairs to Notre Dame Cathedral in Paris in 2022, workers discovered a lead sarcophagus buried deep under the central altar. Analysis by archeologists also found sacred plants for warding off evil heaped inside with the body. Debate continues as to whether the person buried there was a holy man enjoying high honors, or some wicked soul who needed a whole cathedral on top of them to prevent them from becoming a vampire!

CREATING VAMPIRES

When speaking about creating vampires, I will almost exclusively be speaking about undead revenants. At their core, vampires are restless spirits of the dead that are reluctant to pass on, and the spirits of those who die in horrible and abnormal ways may sometimes be reluctant to let go of the land of the living. Most commonly, these types of vampires are created by a violent death. They could have been the victim of a homicide, or they could have had a sudden and unexpected accident. Additionally, any bitter or terrible neighbor might become a vampire, likely because their spirit was restless and mean when they were alive—and that wasn't going to change when they died.

Other times, the smallest misstep in handling a corpse could result in the creation of a vampire. One surprisingly common method of creation in folklore across the globe is if a cat—sometimes another vampire merely in the form of a cat—jumps over a corpse prior to burial, as is the case for the Chinese jiangshi (see page 123). Another way to create a vampire is to splash vampire blood (or in the case of the Macedonian vrykolakas, wine) on the face of a corpse. Likewise, improper burial rites at the gravesite and mistreatment of the spirit after the burial by the living relatives could cause the scorned spirit of the dead to return. Especially as Christianity proliferated through Europe, excommunication or improper burial could lead to an individual coming back from the dead as a vampire. This is partially where the link to holy Christian objects holding power over vampires comes from.

CURSES

Sometimes a person would become a vampire after death because of a curse placed upon them. In Greece, it was thought that anyone denied a Christian burial by a priest was cursed to become a vampire; one could also be cursed by God for committing heresy or perjury. The worst case was a curse cast by a parent on their own child, which was difficult to undo.

Consuming the vampire's flesh, or meat from an animal the vampire has fed on, could also turn a human into a vampire after death. As was the case with Arnold Paole (see page 102), vampirism can be transferred by eating an animal that was killed by a vampire, even after the original vampire is dead. The demonic *rakshasas* of Indian folklore (see page 131) can also transfer their type of vampirism to humans if the human eats the body of the entity.

Sometimes, just being bitten by a vampire was enough to turn a person into one, especially if it killed them. However, it is worth noting that the vampires of folklore rarely want to create more vampires. Sometimes it could be a by-product of their actions, but originally these creatures did not seek out company of their own kind. This may simply reflect the undead's deep obsession with the living.

ELIMINATING VAMPIRES

Vampires were traditionally seen as a menace to the peasantry and working classes, which meant that methods for exterminating them had to be cheap and easily accessible to work. Some combination of brute force, cleverness, and appropriate tools would be necessary for a human to defeat a vampire, and very often it took a whole community working together. Professional vampire hunters like Bram Stoker's Van Helsing were probably rare, but rural communities in Eastern Europe would sometimes raise children suspected of being fathered by a vampire in this role. If a woman's husband died before her pregnancy was apparent, and there were signs of him haunting the house after his burial, then people were likely to suspect that the child was half-human and half-vampire. These dhampir children were thought to be able to see invisible vampires and other monsters, and were valued as a defense against the supernatural. Anyone with religious training was also likely to get roped into a vampire hunt, whether they were a Catholic priest or a Buddhist monk, as the Divine would need to be invoked to defeat evil. The following are the most tried-and-true means of killing vampires that are found in the folklore of different regions.

Beheading

Existing records of vampire hunts and vampire folktales outline the difficulty that a small community might have in trying to figure out the identity of a vampire that was threatening the town. After all, any victims of a direct attack wouldn't live to tell about it, and the diseases spread by the undead left no obvious indication of who was responsible. Once the matter of identity was settled, however, brave locals would form a group to head into the graveyard to dig up and destroy the offender. Beheading and dismembering the vampire corpse was one common approach, and since it left the body otherwise intact when it was buried again, modern archeologists now use it as a clue to figure out which bodies were identified as vampires.

Since most vampires in European stories were bound to their own body (unable to simply steal another), any permanent dismemberment would render the vampire unable to move and crawl out of its grave at night to hunt. At times the head would not only be severed but also placed back in the coffin in a different position; switching the positions of the head and feet was said to make it impossible for the vampire to reassemble. Other options included feeding the head to an animal, or boiling it in wine or vinegar. One drawback to this method is that it would be ineffective against vampires that could simply send their soul flying out to find another corpse to possess, or those (like the *manananggal*, see page 115) who already had detachable heads.

Stake

A stake through the heart is perhaps the most classic means of killing a vampire, though most of us today have forgotten that it matters what kind of wood you use! Hawthorn was any European's first choice for a stake, as the wood of this tree was valued as a ward against vampires and other evil creatures (such as witches). People of Serbian descent in the Balkans claimed that this was the *only* wood that would truly kill a vampire, so it is fortunate that it grows widely across Europe, North

Africa, and parts of the Middle East. For Christians, hawthorn was both the burning bush witnessed by Moses and the crown of thorns worn by Jesus Christ at his crucifixion, lending the tree sacred powers. However, hawthorn's importance probably predates Christianity, as Irish people already held the tree as sacred before their conversion.

Accounts varied as to why stakes were effective against vampires. Some felt that the sacred wood would destroy the vampire's soul when it pierced the heart, while others only saw the stake as a way to permanently imprison the vampire in its coffin by pinning it to its grave (essentially rendering it an ordinary corpse). The latter belief led many people to hammer the stake not only through the vampire's heart but also all the way through the wood at the bottom of the coffin, to make sure the body was fully pinned. In addition to staking the heart with hawthorn, people might take the thorns of the plant and pierce the hands and feet with them, to further "pin" the corpse down and render it harmless. While staking was primarily a European way of exterminating the undead, the practice of putting thorns in the hands and feet was also seen in parts of the Middle East and Asia, suggesting it may have roots in some older, shared custom.

Shrouds, Skins, and Coffins

When vampires are sensitive to sunlight, whatever methods used to stay out of the sunlight are deeply important to them. When all other methods fail, destroying their coffin, shroud, or skin, as in the case of the South American Surinamese *asema*, was the best way to ensure a vampire haunting stopped.

Depending on the period that the vampire died, they were likely to be buried in either a shroud or a coffin. The German shroud eaters (see page 133) were particularly attached to their burial shrouds and there were certain versions of this vampire that required the shroud to be burned with the body to truly eradicate the vampire. The jiangshi (see page 123) must have their coffins burned to ensure prolonged exposure to sunlight and their eventual demise. Some vampires, like the *vrukolak* of northern Dalmatia, in modern-day Croatia, were nailed to the bottom of their coffin to ensure the dead stayed buried.

In other instances, using methods to keep the vampire in their coffin or grave (and therefore out of the hair of the living) was the best solution. Burying the vampire with roses (most commonly dogroses, which is a wild climbing rose native to Europe) could ease the unquiet spirit of the vampire. Wrapping the coffin in a garland of roses could also keep vampires in their coffins. Similarly, throwing a fishing net over the coffin of the Polish *gierach* could keep the vampire in their graves due to the revenant's obsession with untying all the knots of the net.

Fire

When in doubt, fire was an effective weapon against many supernatural foes, including vampires. During the height of the vampire hunts of Eastern Europe, it was standard to first stake the vampire, and then burn them in their coffin to prevent any possibility of their rising again. This approach had the benefit of allowing people to use hawthorn wood for both the stake and the firewood, doubling the opportunities for the tree to work its magic. Modern researchers speculate that the custom of burning vampires originated somewhere in modern-day Bosnia or Türkiye, eventually finding a home alongside the staking method, which may have begun somewhere farther north.

Fire is also an effective means of preventing vampires from being created; since most vampires were corporeal undead tied to their own corpse, they could not rise and terrorize people if they had been cremated down to bones. However, preference for cremation versus burial fluctuated

a great deal in Europe from ancient times to today, in part due to changing religious beliefs. While cremation was a very sanitary means of laying the dead to rest, some Catholic priests began to encourage burial as a way of preserving the body in anticipation of the return of Jesus Christ (who would resurrect the faithful if their bodies were intact). Still, cremation continued in cases where people feared that a regular funeral would not be enough to placate an angry soul. Cremation also maintained popularity as a funerary custom in many parts of Asia, which perhaps accounts for why Asian folklore includes many kinds of vampiric spirits alongside their corporeal counterparts.

Other Methods

Some customs for exterminating vampires changed along with the times. The advent of gunpowder firearms made killing vampires from a distance more feasible than it had been with bows and arrows, and recommendations for shooting vampires spread quickly as farmers acquired these weapons. The earliest firearms were single-shot and took some time to load properly, so choosing effective ammunition was key. People typically resorted to metals with magical properties or bullets that had been blessed in some way. By the nineteenth century, some people preferred to simply fire into a coffin to dispatch a vampire, rather than get close enough to open the lid and stake them.

COINS

Some Slavic folktales from Eastern Europe mention people taking coins and breaking them into shards, which were then fired like bullets from a gun to kill vampires. This custom may have started because some Turkish coins in circulation were minted from silver and had crosses on them (both of which are effective against vampires).

Variations in funeral customs are also reflected in vampire lore. Offering proper burial rites was considered one of the best ways to prevent vampires in the first place, but in some cases a community would hold a funeral retroactively to put a vampire to rest. This approach was used frequently in India and China, while the people of Papua New Guinea would take the bold approach of digging up the bones of a vampiric spirit and bringing them into the home to "adopt" them. In both cases, once the spirits had been given the proper respect and care, they would pass on or become harmless. This approach remained less common in Europe after the spread of Christianity, perhaps due to Church teachings that placed the fate of the soul firmly in God's hands.

Historical Figures and Vampires

The vampires in this chapter are ones for whom we have historical records. Some have been labeled as vampires due to their bloody nature or the fact that they inspired famous vampires of fiction. Others are from firsthand accounts from vampire hunts during the vampire panic of the eighteenth and nineteenth centuries. Some cases of exhumed corpses present a more compelling case for vampirism, while others are more tenuous. Vampires in this section are listed in chronological order to illustrate how the evidence and humanity's understanding of it evolved over time.

VLAD THE IMPALER

Region: Born in Sighişoara, Transylvania; a prince
of Wallachia (in modern-day Romania)
Time: 1376–1431

Vlad III was born in Sighişoara, Transylvania, and was one of
three sons. He was the son of Vlad Dracul, named for his place
in the Christian Order of the Dragon that was meant to protect
Europe from the Turks, who had been invading modern-day
Romania at that time. Dracul, Vlad's father's title, stood for
"dragon," and as Vlad III grew he enjoyed going by Dracula,
or "son of the Dragon." Interestingly, dragons could also be
synonymous with the devil in Romanian folklore, which could
mean that Dracula was also the "son of the devil." As he gained
his own reputation, he was also known as Vlad Tepes (or Vlad

the Impaler). As a child, he was bathed in violence. It's said that he loved watching prisoners being brought up from the castle dungeons to be tortured. In his youth, he had been kidnapped by his father's political rivals for ransom and treated unkindly as a prisoner, rather than as a prince.

His predilection for violence is said to have grown exponentially as Vlad entered adulthood. As his name suggests, he was infamous for his impaling techniques—of which there are many, but most famously, he would place living bodies at the top of stakes driven into the ground and let gravity end his victim's life in anguish. He frequently watched criminals be tortured while eating dinner—with dubious records of him potentially dipping his bread into the blood of one of his victims. His methods of punishment were allegedly so horrendous that crime in Wallachia dropped due to fear of his draconian justice. Accounts place the number of people he personally murdered at a staggering forty thousand to one hundred thousand, depending on the sources. He was ousted by political rivals for his more agreeable brother, but died on the battlefield, where he was beheaded. Later, his body was buried at the island monastery of Snagov.

These accounts, however, were primarily circulated in a fifteenth-century manuscript published in Germany. Some people of Romania have postulated that Vlad Tepes was more of a freedom fighter than a bloodthirsty tyrant. Famously, he (or at least his moniker of Dracula) is the inspiration for Bram Stoker's vampire novel. The folklore of his home region, his bloodthirsty reputation, and his status as Stoker's muse label him as a historical vampire, even if he lacks some of the more mystical qualities of other historical vampires.

ELIZABETH BÁTHORY

Region: Hungary (modern-day Slovakia)
Time: 1560–1614

Elizabeth Báthory, known now as the Blood Countess, lived in Hungary in the 1500s to 1600s and was a countess after she married at thirteen years old. Her husband, Count Ferenc Nádasdy, and her family encouraged her violent nature (her husband's gifts to her were frequently means for torturing their servants under the guise of discipline). When the count died in a war with the Ottoman Empire, Countess Báthory was left a very wealthy widow.

Schooled in violence, the story goes that her truly bloody rampage was kicked off when she was "disciplining" one of her young servant girls. The servant's blood splashed onto her face, and she thought the skin underneath it looked fresher and

more youthful when she wiped it away. Widowed in her castle, Báthory allegedly began drinking and bathing in the blood of young girls and servants to keep up her youthful appearance. Allegedly, she murdered over six hundred servants. Rumors of the extent of her cruelty reached political rivals (who were actually distantly related men in her family displeased with how she kept her husband's wealth and affluence), and she was put on public trial. Hundreds of peasants testified to her bloodlust, but many of them confessed what they heard under torture. Báthory was found guilty, and her punishment was house arrest with a family guardian along with having her title and lands stripped from her and redistributed to her family.

History has labeled her an alleged serial killer, but modern methodologies call her trial into question and historians argue that she (and her reputation) was actually a victim of slander and politicking. For example, the aforementioned torture to receive statements against her: most (if not all) peasants mentioned that they had heard she was murdering people in her castle from friends and servants, rather than stating what they saw directly. Some documents were also presented in court, but they were never officially recorded, which could be due to anything from records lost over time to falsified evidence.

Whether she was legitimately a prolific female serial killer obsessed with capturing youthful vitality through blood or not, her story reflects some of the key themes of vampirism. Although many people maintain Báthory's story is the true inspiration for Bram Stoker's *Dracula* (see page 147), the claim has been debunked. However, it is a tempting hypothesis

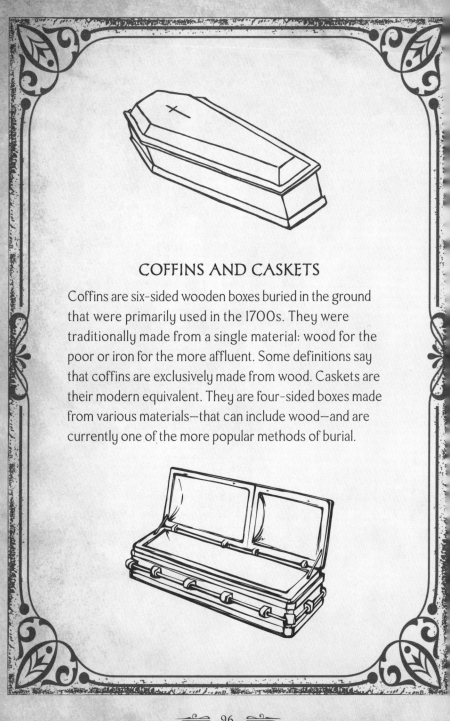

COFFINS AND CASKETS

Coffins are six-sided wooden boxes buried in the ground that were primarily used in the 1700s. They were traditionally made from a single material: wood for the poor or iron for the more affluent. Some definitions say that coffins are exclusively made from wood. Caskets are their modern equivalent. They are four-sided boxes made from various materials—that can include wood—and are currently one of the more popular methods of burial.

and Báthory's bloody story meshes disturbingly well with vampirism. Her obsession with immortal youthful vitality plays into Dracula's ability to appear either old and withered or young and strong. Additionally, her home in Transylvania was where Dracula also made his home, despite the fact that Vlad Dracula was from Wallachia, Romania.

GIURE GRANDO (SOMETIMES SPELLED JURE GRANDO)

Region: Khring, Istria (modern-day Kringa, Croatia)
Time: 1579–1656

While Báthory and Vlad have been immortalized in pop culture as the first vampires, they were labeled as such posthumously and were never considered to be the typical undead vampire. On the other hand, the legend of Giure Grando (if he was a real person) would be the first account of vampirism.

Giure Grando was said to have been a stone mason from a quiet town. There are records of someone with that name dying of illness in 1656, but his vampiric activity wasn't noted until 1672, when a priest was called to deal with his vampiric activity. His haunting began by him knocking on the door of his former home and trying to convince his wife to let him in. When his family fled the area, horrified that his corpse might not be in his grave where they left him, he began knocking on his neighbors' doors instead.

Once the priest arrived, they deemed the activity to be vampiric in nature and led some of the braver men in the village to dig up Grando. Once exhumed, they found that the corpse— while inert—was staring up out of his grave red-faced with a haunting grin. Armed with hawthorn stakes, they tried to stake the vampire and were appalled to find that the stake rebounded off his bloated stomach. After several unnerving attempts, one brave villager managed to behead Grando with a shovel and the vampire let out a death cry that terrified the mob. They burned the body, and a priest said a prayer over the ashes.

What is curious about this folktale is the historic records tied to it and the amount of time that passed between when the body was buried and when it was dug up. In nearly twenty years' time, much of the tissue should have decomposed, yet the accounts of his exhumation track with what is common with much fresher corpses. If the account of Grando is factual and accurate, sceptics might have a harder time explaining away why the body was so well preserved, not to mention smiling. One might wonder what took him so long to get moving . . .

EXHUMATION

"Exhuming" is a term frequently used when speaking of historical accounts of vampirism. It's the act of digging up a ritually buried corpse. Many myths that focus on the eradication of vampires encourage vampire hunters to find a vampire's coffin, destroy a vampire's burial shroud, or keep a vampire away from its place of rest. This reflects the way "real life" vampires were handled by the people they tormented.

PETER PLOGOJOWITZ (ALSO SPELLED PETAR BLAGOJEVIĆ)

Region: Kisilova, Serbia (modern-day Hungary)
Time: 1725

The original report on Plogojowitz's vampiric activity was filed by the Austrian Imperial Army Medical Provisor, Officer Ernst Frombald, recorded in a letter to his superiors in the occupying nation of Austria. Frombald's account includes chilling observations.

Without the tale of his vampirism, Peter Plogojowitz would have been an unremarkable peasant in a rural farming town in Eastern Europe. He had family—a son and a wife—who were both bereaved to see him go, and rattled to see him returned. Ten weeks after Plogojowitz died, he began to rise from the dead and visit people in his community. He asked his wife for shoes (which she refused) and his son for food (which was also not willingly given). The latter act enraged the vampire and he killed his son. His wife was said to be so terrified by the encounter that she fled the village and was never seen again.

Within a week, Plogojowitz allegedly claimed eight other victims—one per night. Each person he visited recounted seeing him hovering over their bed, throttling them in their sleep and sucking their life away. Victims were weak and felt ill the day after their visit and died shortly thereafter. The local villagers called him a *vampyri*, or a spirit back from the dead.

The people of Kisilova called Officer Frombald (who was little more than a kind of Austrian health inspector) to help them deal with the problem, and he enlisted the help of a regional priest. As a mob, the villagers, the priest, and Frombald exhumed Plogojowitz's body. Frombald noted a few peculiarities of the corpse. First, it did not smell like

decay and looked relatively healthy, aside from his nose being gone. While skin had peeled off his body in thin white sheets, the skin that remained looked pink, fresh, and healthy. His nails and hair looked like they had continued to grow posthumously. In fact, his beard appeared fuller . . . and full of fresh blood. The priest deemed Plogojowitz a vampire and staked him in the heart, at which point blood exploded from his chest and gushed out of his mouth and ears. The mob decapitated the body and burned the ashes.

Frombald's report, which was written as a plea for forgiveness for participating in what might be considered an occult ritual, was leaked to a Viennese newspaper called *Wienerisches Diarium*, which published the story on July 21, 1725. Two more attacks followed in Serbian villages in 1726. The story caught on internationally in Germany, England, and France—one French publication embellished the story, saying that victims dreamed of Plogojowitz drinking their blood, and that fresh blood filled his coffin. They also stated that other corpses in the graveyard were protected by garlic and whitethorn.

Plogojowitz is an interesting case because modern medical science can explain away much of the phenomenon (see page 17). The media's coverage and ensuing vampire panic is either the stuff that legends are built on or the beginning of a curious pattern of monsters ripping through the Eastern European countryside.

ARNOLD PAOLE

Region: Medevgia, Serbia
Time: 1726–1731

Arnold Paole (also seen as Arnold Paul and Arnont Paule) was a well-documented case of vampirism. Vampirism was brought to this rural town of Medevgia by Paole, a Serbian soldier who encountered an undead bloodsucker while in Gossowa, Turkish-Serbia. Paole told his neighbors in Medevgia that he had avoided vampirism by eating grave dirt and smearing the vampire's blood on himself.

Later, a tragic freak accident with a cart snapped his neck and killed him. Twenty to forty days later (accounts vary), Paole was seen haunting the living. Four of his neighbors saw him passing through solid doors and windows to drain their life from them in their sleep. Less than three days after seeing the vampiric Paole, all the victims perished. The townsfolk

REVENANTS

Vampires and vampiric spirits would sometimes also be referred to as "revenants" (from the French *revenir*, "to return"). Like vampires, revenants were spirits or animated corpses that would return from the grave to haunt the living or drink blood. The two types of undead seem to have been interchangeable in early folklore.

exhumed the body and saw clear evidence that Paole was a vampire. Despite how long he'd been in the grave, his body had not decayed. Blood oozed out of his orifices—ears, nose, mouth, and eyes—and there was blood on his shirt. Skin and fingernails had fallen off and new ones had grown in their place. Satisfied by the evidence, the mob of townsfolk staked the body, which elicited a groan from the corpse and a spurt of blood. The mob then decapitated all four of Paole's victims and burned their bodies.

Five years later, three Austrian medical officers were called for aid in another bout of vampirism in the same town. The eldest soldier in the village told them Paole's tale and expressed grief and fear over this new vampire murdering his daughter. Three medical officers (Johannes Flückinger, J. H. Sigel, and Johann Friedrich Baumgärten) exhumed a total of thirteen suspected vampires. The bodies were women, children, a servant, and a few soldiers that had been buried in the previous three months. There were various symptoms of vampirism: bloated bodies that used to be skinny; blood coming out of their mouths; fresh skin and nails; and most damming of all—a small red-blue mark found behind the ear labeled as a vampire bite. Some of the exhumed bodies were also in normal states of decay, which added to the perception that something strange was happening.

Flückinger hypothesized that the reason vampires were still causing problems was because Paole had also fed from livestock while a vampire (a sheep or cow, depending on translations). This contaminated the animal with the vampiric disease. Anyone who had eaten the livestock would have become infected too. An account by a Lutheran pastor named Michael Ranft cited "gypsies" (a derogatory term likely referring to Romani nomads) employed as vampire hunters by Flückinger to dispose of the vampire's remains. They did so by decapitating the bodies, burning the remains, and then putting all the ashes into the running water of the Morava River.

Through observations and at least one autopsy, Flückinger created a report titled *Visum et Repertum* ("Seen and Discovered") that was sent to Belgrade and Vienna. Flückinger's report granted scientific validity to the existence of vampires and furthered the vampire craze taking off in Europe. Other journals at the time criticized Flückinger's report as being misleading.

MERCY BROWN

Region: Exeter, Rhode Island, United States
Time: 1892

The tale of Mercy Brown is gruesome, tragic, and one of the earliest tales of vampirism in North America. It predates the publishing of Bram Stoker's *Dracula* by four years as the incidents that transpired were reported on by the local paper, *The Providence Journal Newspaper*, from 1888 to 1892. The Indigenous population of North America did not have many strong vampiric connections in their folklore. The belief in vampires in New England (and North America as a whole) was brought across the sea with the European colonists.

The Brown family consisted of Mercy, the suspected nineteen-year-old vampire; her father, George; her mother, Mary; her elder sister, also named Mary; and Edwin, her younger brother who was eighteen years old. Like many in the region at that time, the Browns were first plagued by tuberculosis, or consumption as it was called at the time. Mary's mother and elder sister contracted the disease first and tragically both perished before 1888. In 1890, her brother Edwin also contracted the disease, followed by Mercy in 1891. Both were weak and unwell, but Mercy was particularly plagued. She would not eat and would wake with blood in her mouth, smearing her bedsheets. She died on January 17, 1892. Her brother enjoyed a brief reprieve from his illness until he got abruptly worse.

George Brown and twelve members of their extended family, remembering Mercy's bloody last days, thought that vampiric activity could be at play and exhumed the corpses of Mercy, her mother, and her sister on March 17, 1892, a mere three months after Mercy had been buried. Her mother and sister were deemed to be appropriately decomposing, but Mercy had rosy cheeks and had even turned over in her grave. When they cut open her body, they found what they thought to be fresh blood still in her heart and liver.

Evidence gathered, the mob of Browns quickly built a fire and burned Mercy's heart. The ashes were mixed with water and given to Edwin to drink in an attempt to lift the curse of his condition. Unfortunately, he died two months later, leaving his father the last survivor of the family.

The myth of Mercy Brown the vampire persists to this day. The cemetery, once named Chestnut Hill, is now colloquially called the Brown cemetery by locals. As recently as 1960, reports of a corpse candle (or bright light containing the spirit of an undead vampire or a living witch) was seen over the gravestone of Mercy Brown. Descendants are told to never touch her gravestone, which once held a pious epitaph that has since been completely erased from the solid stone.

Vampire-Like Creatures across Cultures

This book is an exploration of the different types of vampires in folklore and mythology across cultures. While the stereotypical vampire that we think of is based on the folklore of Eastern Europe, different vampire archetypes are present in folklore of diverse origins. This short directory is alphabetized by entry and dives into several types of vampires in folklore across the globe. I describe their origins, abilities, appearance, and how to best eliminate them. Among these entries are gods, undead revenants, and demons.

TYPES OF VAMPIRES IN FOLKLORE AND MYTHOLOGY

After having defined what makes a vampire a vampire, the following categories of vampire archetypes will help clearly explain the distinct motivations and attributes of each of these vampires. The vampires in this book often fit more than one of these archetypes. These are the vampire archetypes you can expect to see:

Gods: There are at least a few notable deities that require blood as a sacrifice or essential sustenance that helps these gods activate the unparalleled powers they possess. These creatures are considered vampires due to their monstrous nature, supernatural abilities, and predilection for blood.

Demons: A cosmic step down from the divine on the cryptozoological food chain, demons are otherworldly entities that possess psychic or phenomenal powers. Vampires that are classified as demons may be a certain type of demon, or they could be an incorporeal demon that needs to possess a living person or reanimate a corpse to access the breadth of their otherworldly abilities (such as shapeshifting, controlling the weather, influencing animals, and many others). Demons go by many different names across cultures (fey, djinn, yokai, etc.) and I am not exclusively referencing Catholic demons when writing about them.

Undead Revenants: More often than not, vampires in folklore are restless dead that leave their coffin to consume the lifeblood or living essence of the living. This can be a result of a slight to the spirit postmortem or an improper burial.

Ghouls: Ghouls are mindless flesh eaters, and while I hope to draw a distinct line between these creatures and vampires, there are some vampires who feast on flesh as well as blood. For this purpose, ghouls are added as a vampire archetype, but within these pages you will never see a type of vampire with ghoul as their only type.

Monsters: An overwhelming number of vampires are humanoid or from human remains, but there are a few vampiric entities that are more monster than human. Sometimes the monsters even disguise themselves as human to make their hunt for blood a bit easier.

Infanticide Vampires: Many vampires prey exclusively on the blood and life essence of babies and infants. These creatures are often feminine in persuasion.

Femmes Fatales: Similar to the infanticide vampires, these are irresistibly attractive feminine vampires that feast on young men and play on their desires.

Energy or Psychic Vampires: For much of human history, what powered humans was an enigma. Vampires sucking out the life force of the living was usually assumed to be blood due to the aforementioned evidence oozing out of the suspected vampire's mouth looking a lot like blood when the body was exhumed. However, more often than not in folklore, the mystical life-sucking abilities of vampires were usually less linked to blood and more linked to some type of enigmatic psychic energy (much like the astral body referenced on page 26).

Different types of vampires from different cultural origins have different methods of slaying. Take note and be brave.

ALP

Region of origin: Germany
Type: Demon, Undead Revenant

Alps are vampires that appear when an infant dies or is stillborn, and a demon takes up residence in its body. These vampires are powerful shapeshifters, able to assume the form of any animal or a person of any gender. Alps can turn invisible, fly, and spit butterflies and moths from their mouth. This last ability was likely adopted from Eastern European folklore, in which vampires could project their soul from their body in the form of a butterfly. Often, the only way to identify these sneaky vampires is by the white hat that they always wear on their heads.

Alps love to feed on young women, and will creep into their beds at night to sit on their chests and drink their blood; these encounters would be remembered as night terrors or erotic nightmares. This pattern could go on for weeks or months, slowly sickening the woman and driving her mad until she died. When such tempting targets weren't available, alps will feed on cows, horses, and other livestock, eviscerating them or crushing them to death. While these vampires are powerful, they can be warded off with mirrors or magic songs, and if a person can snatch the telltale white hat off their head, they will lose most of their powers. Once an alp is trapped, they can be killed by stuffing a lemon in its mouth and lighting it on fire.

ASEMA

Region of origin: Republic of Suriname
Type: Energy or Psychic Vampire, Demon

Asema are vampires with red eyes and pointed toes that hide during the day in the form of an old woman. At night, they tenderly remove their skin, fold it neatly, and hide it somewhere safe before seeking out blood or energy from unsuspecting victims. They fly as a ball of blue light in the sky until they spy someone with blood that they find exquisite. They must return to their skin before dawn every day because sunlight will destroy them. In their blue light form, they can move through walls, doors, and stone and do not need to be invited in to feast on their victims.

They frequently return to individuals with blood that they enjoy because they are picky eaters—they do not like bitter blood. Red or blue spots at the site of the bite indicate whether an asema has visited a person in their sleep. Consuming herb mixtures or garlic would make a potential victim's blood unpalatable. To ward against these vampires, people would scatter sesame seeds with a single owl talon. Asema are

compelled to pick up and count each small grain and become frustrated and lose count if they pick up the owl talon. While the vampire is distracted in this manner, potential victims try to find the skin and salt it, so the skin will shrink. If it shrinks enough, the vampire will not be able to return to its skin and the sunlight will do the rest.

ASWANG

Region of origin: Philippines
Type: Demon, Femme Fatale, Infanticide Vampire, Undead Revenant

Aswang is the vampire equivalent in the Philippines, although it is not a direct translation and refers to several different types of malevolent creatures that prey on the living. If any of these creatures are encountered, avoidance is the safest route, but many people who believe in these creatures are encouraged to eliminate them on sight. This would be difficult, however, since aswang by nature are shapeshifters. It is rare to see the aswang as anything but an appealing human, even though their true forms can be a bit more monstrous and gruesome.

Two examples, the *mandurugo* and the manananggal, are particularly vampiric.

Manananggal: The manananggal (or the masculine *magtatangal*) is a shapeshifter that can also take the form of a beautiful woman or man. At night, the manananggal will detach its torso from its legs and fly away with large bat wings in search of victims. Their top half leaves their legs at dusk to hunt for blood while the legs (the most vulnerable part of it) stand still. When the top returns at dawn, the creature returns to its normal beautiful and unsuspicious form. The manananggal also has a proboscis tongue and their preferred form of sustenance is fetuses inside pregnant women. There's a version of this creature that is an undead woman who was left at the altar and seeks out husbands-to-be as her primary form of sustenance.

The manananggal can be defeated by salting their legs when their top half is away. Some versions of this creature (that go by many names, but most similarly a *krasue*) are only the heads and internal organs flying away with bat wings on their head.

Mandurugo: The mandurugo is the closest translation to a vampire in Filipino folklore. This bloodsucker usually takes the form of a beautiful young woman who drinks

her unsuspecting victim's blood through a proboscis in her tongue (usually when her victims are peacefully asleep and otherwise helpless). The creature has feathered wings on the shoulders and hips.

An old folktale called "The Girl with Many Loves" tells the story of a young and beautiful woman (secretly a mandurugo) who marries, one after the other, five large and healthy men who all die mysteriously in their sleep after wasting away to nothing. Her final husband, fearing for his life, feigns sleep with a knife under his pillow. When he feels a prick in his neck, he stabs the creature, and he hears a shriek and a fluttering of wings. The next morning, his wife is found stabbed by the same knife, meaning that she was sucking the life from her husbands to keep herself youthful. A different version of this creature is a *kinnara* or *kinnari* (which can sometimes take the form of a beautiful young man or woman) who remains devoted to their significant other until the mortal breaks their heart.

BHUTA

Region of origin: India
Type: Demon, Infanticide Vampire, Ghoul, Undead Revenant

Certain versions of the bhuta (sometimes anglicized as *boota*) are more ghoul-like or akin to a zombie than a vampire. Bhutas are shadowy-looking spirits that inhabit corpses of people who died in the following ways: violent, shocking, or untimely deaths; suicide; or those who died with a deformity.

The shadow creature, or bhuta, will reanimate the corpse. At this point, the bhuta can be identified by its lack of shadow. Usually, it will stay in the graveyard and consume corpses— along with any living human that has the misfortune of wandering into their path—but they will also travel to places that they frequented when they were alive. If hungry enough, it will also drink milk and the blood of infants. Burning turmeric will keep them away and they will leave people alone if they're lying down (because they can no longer rest). It's hard to tell whether a bhuta is more an undead revenant or a demonic spirit reanimating a corpse. Based on the presence of the shadow creature and the bhuta's foul aura that can repel animals, it could be a nonhuman entity (further supported by its ability to shapeshift into a bat or an owl). But the fact that they will visit the corpse's old haunts suggests it could be an undead revenant.

No matter their vampiric archetype, some communities revere them, in a sense. Altars are built for bhutas, complete with a comfy place for it to rest (that they are unlikely to use), food, and fresh milk. These offerings are meant to appease the monster and keep it from spreading illness and plague to the living.

CIHUATETEO

Region of origin: Aztec Empire (modern-day Mexico)
Type: Femme Fatale, Infanticide Vampire, Undead Revenant

The undead revenant version of a *cihuateteo* is the reanimated corpse of a woman who died in childbirth or birthed a stillborn baby. She attacks children and drains their lives as recompense for the life that was stolen from her. These attacks historically were connected to illness, citing the cihuateteo returning night after night to suck life from children as they slept until they were dead. While feared and terrifying, these creatures can be staved off by leaving bits of meteorites or bits of bread around a cradle to protect newborns. The cihuateteo will consider these a peace offering and will leave the newborn alone.

Other Aztec legends call this creature a *civateteo* or a *cihuateotl*. This version of the creature is most frequently seen at crossroads after the sun sets . . . right before she pounces on her victims with a paralytic bite. There are records and sightings of them flying through the jungle and preying on men at crossroads up until the 1500s. These creatures are also the handmaidens to Tlazolteotl, the goddess of sexuality, vice, filth, and adulterers. They are also emissaries from Mictlan, the lowest level of the underworld in Aztec mythology.

DHAMPIR

Region of origin: The Balkans
Type: Demon-like

Also known as a *dhampiresa* (for a female version of this creature), *vampirdžia* (in Macedonian), *sâbotnik* (another name in Balkan folklore), or *glog* (in Bulgarian), a dhampir is a little different from most other vampires. Dhampirs are created by the unholy union of a vampire and a living creature (most frequently their widow) and many potential dhampirs are stillborn. Dhampirs can also be born during the unclean days between Christmas and New Year's, when proper Christian birth rites could not be performed on newborns.

These hybrids have none of the powers of the vampire and have bones made of a rubbery, cartilage-like substance rather than proper bones. Their parentage—and the fact that they could steal a living human's bones to become fully human—usually means they are generally distrusted and live the life of a vagabond. They live dramatically shorter lives than humans and are at higher risk of becoming a vampire when they die. In spite of this, they possess the unique ability to see vampires for what they truly are, which is especially helpful if they can turn invisible or shapeshift. They can eradicate a vampire with any tool, which is why they are destined to be ideal vampire hunters. They also know other magical rituals that help ward off vampires, notably putting their clothes on backwards, looking through their shirtsleeves to detect any undead shenanigans, or whistling to ward off the undead.

DRAUGR

Region of origin: Scandinavia
Type: Ghoul, Undead Revenant

Pinning down exactly what the ancient Norse believe about anything is difficult, at best, although the presence of several different types of powerful, violent, undead revenants are indisputable in mythology. There's a draugr, who is a mean and mighty undead revenant that behaves similarly to a dragon. Draugrs keep a hoard of treasure that they accumulated in life and will slaughter and suck the life out of anyone who gets close. They're said to have otherworldly strength and can grow to two or three times their normal size. They can control the weather and may use this to menace their community. They can also shapeshift into many forms, but most frequently they turn into a cat and slink into houses. Once inside, they sit on the chest of one of the residents and increase their mass until they suffocate, which is how they drain their victims' life force. Residents can trap these vampires by tying their toes together so they can't move or placing straw around their graves in a counterclockwise pattern.

A *drauge* (also known as a *haugbui* or "sleeper in the mound") has all the powers of the draugr, but cannot leave their burial mound. Avoidance is the best course of action when encountering them. When Christianity started proliferating through Norse societies, another common way to defeat all vampires was to rebury them in a Christian cemetery with Christian burial rites. Beheading and burning the body is also a method of disposal.

GIENGANGER

Region of origin: Modern-day Germany or Denmark
Type: Energy or Psychic Vampire, Undead Revenant

Also sometimes called a *gienfärd*, this vampire shows up in the research the brothers Grimm conducted while compiling folklore stories in the early 1800s for their book *Grimms' Tales for Young and Old*. It also shows up in the *Poetic Edda*, which is one of the oldest written records of compiled poetry from ancient Norse society.

Most commonly, these vampires are reanimated corpses of the murdered or murderers. Their violent ends (or violent lives) may inspire a soul to try to reanimate their corpse—due to either unfinished business from a life cut short or the fear of what would face them in the afterlife. Giengangers haunt their families and sustain themselves off the fear they inspire. They are similar to drauges (see above), but do not have the same supernatural strength and can leave their graves. The methods of eliminating drauges work for giengangers, too.

A gienganger is a soul returned to its flesh-and-bone body past the time of its usefulness, likely from entering a pact

SEDUCTION

Vampires are creatures of seduction in both fiction and folklore. This stems from a postmortem phenomenon where the bloating of a corpse could also make the undead seem more virile than they actually were. When corpses were exhumed and people told stories of male vampires with an erection in their coffin, vampire folklore evolved to depict vampires trying to seduce their wives.

with a powerful, otherworldly entity or the devil (depending on the period). This particular iteration of the German vampire revolves around the belief that the soul is a very real thing, in spite of its intangibility. Souls of the dead generally want to pass on to the afterlife when their corporeal body dies, and sticking around impedes the natural process of a soul entering the afterlife. This hiccup in the laws of nature creates the revenant.

JIANGSHI

Region of origin: Siberia, Mongolia, and China
Type: Undead Revenant

These Chinese vampires are made either when a person dies far from their home or when a cat jumps over the dead body prior to burial. They have long white hair; curved, clawlike fingernails; fluorescent green-white skin; luminous red eyes; and serrated teeth—rather than the fangs we normally associate with vampires. They also must escape their grave before they're buried, because once they're entombed, they cannot leave, and they may use their deadly, plague-ridden breath to escape. Blind, the jiangshi scents its prey while in either human or wolf form. It also has the ability to fly as a mote of blue-white light in the sky. It likes the taste of the blood of men and is described as a virile vampire—sexually assaulting bodies while they devour their prey.

The moon is where this vampire draws power, so it will hide during daytime or during a new moon. It is at its most powerful during a full moon. Garlic or a line of small iron shavings will ward against this vampire. It is also sensitive to thunder and loud noises and can be chased off with the sound of drums. It cannot cross running water. It is compelled to pick up and count small scattered objects, so throwing fistfuls of red peas or rice will slow the vampire down. If one can lure the vampire back to its grave (potentially with a trail of small objects) it will be trapped there. Adhering a Buddhist or Daoist death blessing note to their forehead will also render their powers inert, and proper burial rites must be performed to bind the vampire to its grave.

KERES

Region of origin: Greece
Type: Demon, Undead Revenant

Daughters of Nyx, the goddess of the night, *keres* (*ker* in the singular) are spirit-like entities that answer to the Fates (three ancient Greek divinities that control the life, death, and destiny of every mortal human). They seek out souls slated to die violent, bloody, or painful deaths with a vampiric thirst, but obey the word of the Fates and only feed from people the Fates allow. They are usually described as dark-skinned women with blood-red robes that fly on leathery black wings. As a flock, they siphon life and blood from their victims with white fangs and clawlike nails.

One of their favorite haunts is a bloody battlefield. Keres let out bloodcurdling shrieks before they suck the life and blood out of fallen soldiers. In the *Iliad* and other epic poems or stories from ancient Greece, keres would desperately try to distract heroes on the battlefield in hopes of changing their fates. So much so that gods would swat them away and protect their favored human heroes from these mosquito-like spirits. Seeing a ker off the battlefield harbingered disease, old age, and death.

LILITH

Region of origin: Mesopotamia (modern-day Iraq)
Type: Demon, Femme Fatale, God, Infanticide Vampire

Lilith has existed since 4000 BCE in many different iterations across cultures. The Mesopotamian cultures of Sumer, Akkadia, Assyria, and Babylon all had renditions of a malicious and bloodthirsty demoness that ate babies, drank the blood of men, and was the most fearsome of each of the pantheons (see page 33). Records of a lilitu spirit haunting crossroads are reminiscent in the mythology of Sumer, one of the oldest cultures in the world. Ancient Babylonians knew her as the goddess Lamashtu or as a lesser demoness. The ancient Assyrians called demonesses *lilats* who stole babies and drank their blood. To the Greeks, she was Lamia, a queen forced to kill her children for her lover's infidelity. The Dead Sea Scrolls and Jewish folklore named her Lilith and her demon children were called the lilim. Other monikers include Bat Zurgem Bogey-Wolf, Chief of the Succubi, Daughter of the Night, the Devil's Consort, Flying One, Foolish Woman, Maid of Desolation, Princess of Demons, Queen of Hell, and most ominously: the Ancient.

With a wide breadth of material to draw on, I feel compelled to highlight a few points about this mother of monsters. Because there are many different versions of Lilith around the world, there are opportunities where prescribing her the same significance across cultures (i.e., calling her the same entity) is a dubious practice at worst and difficult to substantiate at best. There are certain sources that link the

Assyrian and Babylonian versions of Lilith to the one of Jewish folklore, but the connection is contested in academic circles. Likewise, it may be considered a stretch linking her Greek iteration back to those of Mesopotamia.

Empusa

Empusas are vampires that are closer to demons. Aside from their connection to Lilith, they are also said to be handmaids to the Greek goddess of magic and witchcraft, Hecate. Shapeshifters with mind-altering powers, the empusa may actually be a beautiful woman or just the illusion of one. They seek out young men, offering them illusions of wealth and grandeur, to tempt their prey to stay docile and loving while they drain their life energy and/or their blood. One fictional tale called *The Life of Apollonius* tells the story of a young scholar who falls in love with a rich woman from out of town who lavishes him with comforts the likes of which he has never known. A wise and astute mentor notices the holes in her illusion (he can't interact

with any of her servants and while the food looks decadent, it tastes bland) and once the cracks are noticed, the entire ruse falls apart and the fiancée reveals herself to be an empusa. These vampires are slow and are only successful in trapping their prey if the illusion of their comforts is not dispelled.

Lamashtu

Also known as Dimme to the Sumerians, the Babylonian Lamashtu is a monstrous goddess that is more monster than human. As the goddess who oversees the deaths of the young, balances the population through disease, and destroys crops, she is considered the most malicious of the Babylonian pantheon. Hungry for violence and one with a voracious appetite, she is the bane of new babies and pregnant mothers, as those are her favorite meals. Most of the information uncovered about Lamashtu are prayers and spells to keep her way from newborns and children.

Lamia, the Queen

There are a few distinct Lamias that Lilith can be linked to.
Firstly, Lamia was a first-century Greek woman who appeared
in the writings of Diodorus Siculus. Greek mythology
surrounding her states that she was one of the most beautiful
human (or demigoddess, depending on the accounts) consorts
of the king of the gods, Zeus, and was mother to many of
his children. When Zeus's wife, Hera, discovered his affair,
she murdered all of Lamia's children. The Roman retelling of
Lamia's tale has a slightly more horrendous ending where Hera
forced Lamia to eat all of her children while cursing her with
immortality and eyes that remain open. In both versions, Lamia
is driven mad by her grief and she must sustain herself on the
blood and flesh of illegitimate children.

Lamiae, the Monsters

Also known as a "leacher" or "swallower" in Greek, these
female vampires primarily seek out children. It is unclear
based on the mythology whether the *lamiae* are children
of Queen Lamia or whether they are simply entities
that followed in Lamia's footsteps. These lamiae have an
unquenchable thirst for the blood of children and are most
frequently portrayed as half-serpent, half-woman with
shockingly beautiful eyes.

Lilith and the Lilim

Although the legitimacy of this claim is put into question (its
earliest record is in the tenth century CE), Jewish folklore—
particularly that of the Middle Ages—named Lilith the first
wife of Adam. In the tale, she was made from the same clay

as Adam, rather than from his ribs. Once she refused to obey him, she was cast out of the Garden of Eden and went to live with a demon named Samael. God then cursed her to have a hundred demon children a day. Whether it was her marriage to a demon, becoming the mother of demons, or being cursed by God, Lilith developed an insatiable bloodlust and is often portrayed as either a malignant force or a trickster goddess in old Jewish folklore. In the Bible, she is also depicted as a screech owl, snake, or sea monster.

Lilitu

The lilitu is first mentioned in the Epic of Gilgamesh (a Sumerian poem dating back to as early as 2100 BCE) as a demoness living in a tree. As such, lilitus are frequently seen in wild places. They are said to be seductresses that lurk outside of men's homes. If they succeed, they copulate with the man and then drink his blood until he dies. The connection between the Sumerian (and subsequently, the Babylonian) lilitu and its Hebrew iterations is difficult to substantiate, but the dates and cross-cultural exchange are close enough that there may be some overlap.

RAKSHASAS

Region of origin: India
Type: Demon, Femme Fatale

The Vedas, the sacred texts of Hinduism, have stories of demonic demigods called rakshasas. They were originally crafted to protect the source of eternal life, but they're the embodiment of all the worst traits of humans (greed, deceit, lust, and violence) and, as such, did not make very good guardians. They are described as being covered in blood, having five legs, and having oddly portioned animal and human parts. They have fangs, shapeshifting abilities, poisonous claws that kill a human with a single touch, and sometimes other magical powers as well. Their eyes, no matter what the form, are vertical slits, but they can otherwise change their shape so that they are either beautiful and irresistible or meek and unassuming.

These creatures hunt humans for sport and drain their blood. Female rakshasas seduce men into the jungle and then drain them of their blood. Male rakshasas hide in trees and drop down to suck the life out of pregnant women. Eating rakshasa flesh can cause insanity or illness. Rakshasas enjoy tormenting the living, relaxing in cemeteries, and ruining religious rituals.

They are difficult to identify. Once found, they can be trapped in the sun for several hours and will then be reduced to ash. If a rakshasa is pestering a person, calling them "uncle" will make them fade away. It is worth noting that there are "good" rakshasas that do not relish the torment of humans, but they are few and far between.

SHROUD EATER

Region of origin: Germany
Type: Energy or Psychic Vampire, Ghoul, Undead Revenant

A common burial practice in much of Europe during the Middle Ages (and beyond—especially for rural peoples) was to bury their dead not in a coffin, but rather to wrap the body in a burial shroud. This was true for Muslims and the people of the Ottoman Empire as well as a key component in Egyptian ritual embalming. Unlike ancient Egyptian bodies, however, the bodies of Europeans in the Middle Ages were not embalmed.

Shroud eater is an umbrella term for many different types of German vampires—including *begierig, dodelecker, nachttoter, nachtzer, nachzehrer,* and *neuntöter*—that have a ghoulish unending hunger, but are nevertheless considered vampires. Shroud eaters (as you may have guessed) eat their burial shrouds in their graves. One of these vampires, the begierig, even loosely translates to "avid chewer." Wasting away in their graves chewing incessantly on their shrouds until the linen is completely gone, they only rise after the shroud is consumed to begin eating itself, other corpses in the graveyard, or the flesh of family members.

Many of these shroud eaters have an almost campy quality to them—some folklore says that they'll tie the tails of cows together in the field for amusement. They're also depicted in ways that don't inspire the same horror of other vampires. They are inert during the day, and when exhumed they can be identified by having one eye open wide in their grave, one thumb removed from their hand clutched in the other fist, and their shroud between their lips. At their most fearsome they are nocturnal hunters that can suck the psychic energy from their families from their graves. They are considered prolific plague carriers and extreme caution is impressed upon those digging up suspected shroud eaters as they have terrible breath that can kill a person.

Some of them (like the dodelecker) are more beast than human once they are reanimated, and shamble and moan rather like a zombie. Others are a bit closer to a type of demonic entity (such as the nachzehrer) and have shapeshifting abilities that are used more for avoiding people than to trick or harm them. Sprinkling the more intelligent shroud eaters with small grains of rice is an excellent way to trap the vampire in their grave all night, because they are compelled to pick up each grain and count them before lurking on members of their former community. They are also supposedly skittish, do not like being seen, and are easily spooked by loud noises.

As this is an undead vampire, there are many ways for them to be made, most notably by drowning or being buried in clothes that weren't owned by the deceased. Luckily, it is prohibitively difficult for many of the different types of shroud eaters to make any more of their kind. Unlike other vampires, shroud eaters rarely balloon out of control as a problem for a town.

They do not like garlic and a vampire hunter's inclination to employ hawthorn wood is well used here. Staking or beheading are sound methods of eliminating the vampire. If the goal is to lay the soul to rest, spreading hawthorn brambles around the grave will also keep them from leaving their grave. Tying the mouth closed with clean white linen can also stop these vampires from menacing their family any longer.

STRYX OR STRIX

Region of origin: Ancient Greece
Type: Demon, Femme Fatale, Monster

Greek mythology was well known by the hoi polloi (or common folk), so when the Roman Empire sought to conquer the Greeks, they also integrated their mythologies. The same creatures and divine entities often show up in both mythologies with different names and slight alterations to their stories. We can see this with the stryx or strix of ancient Greece and the *striga* or *strigae* of ancient Rome.

Slight variations occur in both, but they are either an undead spirit masquerading as a living entity, or a living witch with wild powers and an insatiable thirst. They often take

the form of an old woman during the day and can shapeshift into an owl with the face of an old woman. At night they transform into their winged shape or travel as a white mote of light in the sky to either meet up with others of their kind or feast upon children.

During medieval witch hunts, this visage was one that was used to inspire the eradication of witches. However, the mythology indicated that they were powerful and could curse individuals that opposed them (which the old ladies who were tried as witches rarely did). Leaving offerings of chicken hearts, black lambs, puppies, or honey cakes could endear villagers to them and would offer them protection from these demon curses and their thirst.

VAMPIRE

Region of origin: Various
Type: Undead Revenant

Vampire (and the Dutch derivative, *vampyre*) was first penned as the "correct" spelling of the many different terms and spellings for the word in 1734. The term itself is Serbian in nature, as are many of the attributes and traits that we now associate with vampires. Here are other similar terms that popped up in Europe and their unique vampire variations.

Upior: (Polish) Derived from the term for sorcerer, upiors are a type of shroud eater that lurks at crossroads and pounce on their victims. Suspected upiors are burnt and the ashes fed to children upon reaching puberty to prevent them from becoming vampires. Inflamed upiors can explode into maggots and can't be truly dealt with until all the bugs are burned.

GOD FORSAKEN

Excommunication from the Church is an expulsion and barring from the physical building and communities, but also a removal of the protections that God offers. People can be posthumously excommunicated from the Church after suicide or for improper burial practices. Excommunicated individuals were at high risk of becoming vampires.

Upir: (Polish, Russian) The result of a suicide or violent death, the upir controls all the water in a region and can suck all the water out of crops and bodies of water. An aspen wood stake to the heart, pinning the upir to their coffin in a single blow, can render them powerless.

Vampiir: (Estonian, Lettish, Finnish, Russian, Swedish, Ukrainian) Active only at the darkest part of the night, these vampires can shapeshift into bats or wolves and skulk into victims' homes to smother them in their sleep. They do not like the sun and can be vanquished by fire and decapitation.

Vampir: (German) Undead revenants of heretics and murder victims with clawlike nails and a bloated rubbery body, vampirs are weak to silver and garlic and can dissolve to ash if staked in the heart.

Vampirdzhija: (Bulgarian) This term describes a vampire/human half-breed with red eyes that can stake vampires with thorns.

Vampyri: (Austrian) Ernst Frombold used this word to describe the exhumed vampire Peter Plogojowitz (see page 99).

VRYKOLAKA

Region of origin: Greece, Macedonia, Türkiye
Type: Demon, Undead Revenant

When it comes to oral tradition, or tales that are passed down from word of mouth over generations, things can be difficult to track. Such is the case with the *vrykolak, vrykolakas, vroucolaca,* or *vrykolaka.* Each of these versions originates from a different area and has distinct lore associated with it. Vrykolaka, in particular, are usually linked to werewolves—some versions of the vampire are a corpse reanimated by the soul of a dead werewolf. Vrykolaka even means "wolf fairy" in some Greek translations.

Some are created when a cat jumps over a body, others when wine or blood is splashed upon the corpse's face. Early perceptions of these vampires saw them as restless souls to be cared for. Finishing their business, which could be as simple as cleaning the house or running an errand, would calm the vrykolaka and stop the haunting. When the Greek Orthodox Church began gaining popularity, excommunication from the church and improper burial rites resulted in vrykolaka, and the creature required a proper Christian burial. The Greek Orthodox Church tied these restless spirits to the Christian devil and labeled them as evil. Around this time, it was said that they would haunt people they knew—either sucking their life away or having relations with their widow.

Traditional methods of beheading, staking the body to the ground, and burning the remains with a Greek Orthodox priest presiding over the ceremony would eradicate the vrykolaka.

Vampires in fiction

The vampires in this chapter are far removed from the folklore that inspired them, but they keep the legends alive. From the folk story of Sava Savanović and the King of the Night to the Byronic vampires of *True Blood* and *Buffy the Vampire Slayer*, the following vampires show what has made bloodsuckers so popular. Exhuming the roots of folklore in each of these fictional vampires shows how what it means to be a vampire has changed over the centuries. How humanity treats the dead is more telling of what they think of the living.

SAVA SAVANOVIĆ AND *AFTER NINETY YEARS* BY MILOVAN GLIŠIĆ (1880)

Sava Savanović is the most famous vampire in the folklore of the Balkan region of Eastern Europe and remains the center of superstition even today among the older generations. Savanović was said to haunt an old flour mill in Zarožje, Serbia, which has served as a kind of impromptu tourist attraction for those well informed and brave enough to find it. Savanović's tale of terror was immortalized by author Milovan Glišić in his novella *After Ninety Years* (1880), which preserved the vampire's legend in an appealing style that honors the rural culture of Serbia in the late nineteenth century.

After Ninety Years begins as something of a love story, with a young man named Strahinja (pronounced Strakh-in-ya) losing hope that he will ever win approval to marry the girl he loves, Radojka. Strahinja packs his bags to leave town, only to overhear the local elders discussing how yet another man assigned to oversee the flour mill has been strangled to death, and no one else will volunteer. He boldly steps up to take the job and prepares to ambush whatever creature might be haunting the mill. Strahinja starts the mill up again, and then arranges a log under a blanket in front of the fire, while hiding in the rafters with a loaded gun. Then Sava Savanović, "red as blood," enters silently wrapped in a burial shroud. When he attacks the form in front of the fireplace and finds only a log, he curses himself, revealing his name before Strahinja shoots him. The next day Strahinja brings news of the vampire to the villagers, who immediately take up arms and begin the hunt. They eventually locate Savanović's grave and destroy him; in gratitude for saving the town, the villagers strong-arm Radojka's father into allowing the lovebirds to marry.

All's well that ends well, in the book at least. But in the film adaptation *Leptirica* ("she-butterfly," 1973), Savanović's soul manages to escape from his coffin in the guise of a butterfly. On his wedding night, poor Strahinja finds a mark on Radojka's body that was not there before, in the same place that Savanović was staked. Realizing his wife has become the vampire's new host, he attempts to destroy Savanović once and for all, but the film ends with the two destroying one another.

Though he is immortalized in literature and film, Sava Savanović is truly a vampire legend that has survived hundreds of years of retellings. Though his mill may have crumbled, his name lives on today as a warning not to trust the little butterflies that float on the breeze.

Folklore Sources Referenced

The entirety of *After Ninety Years* is an adaptation of a popular folktale of the time. However, the book also preserves a number of vampire superstitions and related customs that might otherwise have been lost to time (the idea that Slavic vampires can eject their soul from their body in the form of a butterfly being one example). Glišić's text mentions the special properties attributed to mill water, Turkish *marjas* (coins), and towels, and shows how a black stallion was used to help detect the vampire's unmarked grave.

Cultural Context

Sava Savanović is still not well known in English-speaking countries, and Glišić's novella was not translated into English until 2015, meaning it had no influence on writers like Stoker and Le Fanu, whose work came out around the same time. However, Savanović remains a favorite in Serbia and Croatia, and was even the subject of a public feud when the towns of Zarožje and Valjevo both proclaimed him to be their tourism mascot. Although the mill featured in the story collapsed in 2012, public funds were raised to restore it as a landmark in 2019.

CARMILLA BY JOSEPH SHERIDAN LE FANU (1872)

A Gothic horror published in 1872, *Carmilla* by Joseph Sheridan Le Fanu is the story of the friendship and haunting between the narrator, a Victorian teen named Laura, and the immortal revenant vampire Carmilla. Set in Austria, it shows

BYRONIC VAMPIRE

Polidori's 1819 short story "The Vampyre" essentially rebranded the vampire as it was seen by the public. At the time, due to the tales of Arnold Paole (see page 102) and Peter Plogojowitz (see page 99), vampires were thought of as fearful undead creatures potentially invading London and western Europe. Painting his vampire, the posh yet mysterious Lord Ruthven, as an aristocratic figure with unfortunately irredeemable habits, entranced the public.

A Byronic hero is a romantic hero in works of fiction that is named after a friend of William Polidori's, the poet Lord Byron. It is a character archetype of a proud yet moody cynic and contrarian who is consistently deeply miserable despite the pleasures of life his aristocracy grants him. There is usually something that he wishes to seek vengeance for (a rake of an ex-friend, a greater injustice, or a familial qualm), and potentially redemption, which makes him capable of deep love.

The Byronic vampire is just as romanticized as his heroic counterpart, but his vices and flaws fly closer to villainy as a by-product of arrogance and aristocratic upbringing. The Byronic vampire amplifies these attributes and can be seen in its modern pop culture iteration, affectionately named as the antithesis of the "Manic Pixie Dream Girl"— the "Depressive Demonic Nightmare Boy."

a deep and intimate friendship blossoming between the two main characters while Carmilla acts increasingly more bizarre and reports circulate of a mysterious illness sweeping through young girls in a nearby town.

While Carmilla sleepwalks at night and Laura develops the same inexplicable illness that is claiming the country girls, the tertiary characters attempt to save both. Carmilla is unveiled as a vampire who has habitually seduced and murdered several young girls throughout the century. The end of the novella follows Laura and her father teaming up with the vengeful father of one of Carmilla's earlier victims, and they stake the vampire in her coffin.

Folklore Sources Referenced

Both Le Fanu and Stoker were inspired by a study done in 1751 by a French abbot named Antoine Augustin Calmet called *Treatise on the Apparitions of Spirits and on Vampires or Revenants of Hungary, Moravia, et al*. One section differentiates between true resurrections (which are only performed by God) and what happens when a vampire leaves its grave. This differentiation separates the soul of a vampire from the holiness of God and is why at one point in the novella, when Laura sings a hymn for one of the dead girls, Carmilla has a rageful outburst about how the song hurts her sensitive ears.

Cultural Context

Carmilla is the first instance of a lesbian vampire. Laura's horror and attraction to Carmilla reflect the same underlying message—that something about both vampirism and loving a woman seems wrong, yet difficult to resist. This set a

SUBTLE SILVER

Silver is at the root of several odd quirks of vampirism. From 1835 to 1940, silver was placed behind glass to give mirrors their reflective quality. From 1727 to 1950, silver nitrate was also used as an agent in film cameras to darken images onto film when exposed to light. One reason that vampires may not appear in film or in mirrors is not because of their lack of a soul, but rather because of the silver used in both items. Curious that two easy ways of quickly identifying vampires were both phased out in the same decade, no?

precedence for later works of vampire fiction to be a safe haven of expressing queerness, with examples as early as the Lambert Hillyer film *Dracula's Daughter* (1936), which blends the stories of *Dracula* and *Carmilla*. The thesis of the film links vampirism to lesbianism—an incurable and uncontrollable sinful urge that goes against God. Modern lesbian vampires are much less steeped in shame, nor do they have the same forbidden symbolism.

DRACULA BY BRAM STOKER (1897)

Bram Stoker's epistolary horror novel published in 1897 really kicked off vampires in popular literature. It follows the unmasking and subsequent vanquishing of a Transylvanian vampire, the titular Count Vlad Dracula, after he goes on a murderous rampage in England. Jonathan Harker, a young solicitor who is Dracula's first victim, and his new wife, Mina, team up with an esoteric doctor and vampire hunter named Professor Abraham Van Helsing, as well as a few other men who lost the woman they were courting (and Mina's best friend), Lucy, to Dracula's hunger. Seeking vengeance, this group embarks on a quest to save themselves from the vampiric disease and their home from the invasion of this monstrous entity. It is told through letters, journal entries, receipts, ship logs, and other found documentation.

A charming aristocrat who uses affluence and money acquired over a millennia as a means of control would be a villain even without his superhuman strength and other supernatural talents, but with them, the protagonists are continually flummoxed and bested by Dracula throughout the novel. Dracula has the ability to shapeshift into wolves,

rats, and birds of prey. Both in these forms and in the form of a man, he can control these animals. He has psychic powers and can consume energy and blood from his victims without entering the room—sometimes only appearing as a black cloud or fine mist. Although the two are never explicitly linked, the strange storms and anomalous weather patterns that follow the Count suggest that he also has the ability to control the weather. Ingesting the blood of a vampire creates another vampire and the vampires he makes (his brides) are fiercely loyal to him.

With the guidance and wisdom of Professor Van Helsing, the group of protagonists learn the Count's weaknesses and develop a plan for tracking down and eradicating the terror. They learn that he cannot use his powers from dawn to dusk (for the most part), although he does walk in the sunlight and conducts business in London during the day without his supernatural abilities. As such, much of their machinations to defeat the Count are performed during the day, when he needs to go to ground (or sleep in his coffin, lined with soil from his home in Transylvania). He also cannot cross running water unless in his coffin, which is one way they track his movements. The vampiric disease (sometimes also called a curse) is kept at bay by garlic, holy water, and silver coins, but cannot ultimately be cured by them.

Stoker based the character off of folklore, historical figures, and likely some themes of sexual frustration. Much of the vampire lore that is popularized today can find its roots in Stoker's seminal work, so we can be thankful that he was thorough in his research.

Folklore Sources Referenced

Eastern European folklore—particularly in areas around present-day Romania, Serbia, Bulgaria, and Moldova—can be seen in *Dracula* in myriad ways. The way vampirism is transferred was likely sourced from an article on Transylvanian superstitions, which states that vampires can turn other humans into vampires by drinking their blood and killing them. Bulgarian folklore connects the soul to our reflections and could be why Dracula's reflection is notably absent. Bloodsucking is rather ubiquitous in vampire folklore, but Romanian vampires were said to draw blood from their victims' throats. There was an old folktale of a handsome strigoi who beguiled a young girl to fall in love with him. They were wed, then later her parents were scandalized when they thought they saw the newlyweds copulating through an open window and were subsequently horrified when they realized he was draining her blood through her throat.

Stoker mostly based Count Dracula on Eastern European folklore, but the vampiric myths that he referenced were not exclusively in that area. For example, some of his earliest research makes note of a *penanggalan*, a Malaysian vampire that is the floating head of a woman trailing her guts and hunting down babies to drink, which is believed to be some of the inspiration for Dracula's brides. Additionally, the belief that vampires cannot cross running water is from the Greek vrykolaka (see page 138), where vampire hunters in Greece would dig up and then rebury suspected vampires on remote islands to protect their homes.

Conversely, there are many hints that Dracula is more demon than an immortal blood drinker raised from the dead, but he could potentially be an amalgamation of both. Dracula's aversion to holy symbols divorces him from the Christian God. I've mentioned previously that a potential cause for vampirism is excommunication and violent death. Moreover, the drive to infect others with his vampiric disease demonstrates a demon's desire to lure more souls away from the Christian God. His shapeshifting ability, dominion over weather, superhuman strength, incorporeal form, and psychic powers align with the prerogatives of a demon rather than an immortal corpse thirsting for blood.

Demonology aside, the methods for killing a vampire that are employed by the characters in Stoker's novel (stakes through the vampire's heart, a mouth full of garlic, decapitation, and burning the corpse) are all aligned more with the methods of eighteenth-century European vampire hunters. Dracula's inability to use his powers during the day reflects the fact that ancient real-life vampire hunters would discover vampires sleeping powerless in their coffins. For a fictional vampire, the creator is entitled to craft a compelling villain for their stories. Stoker's vampire is an amalgamation of lore and is impossible to classify into a single vampiric category.

Cultural Context

Dracula is the dark father of modern vampires. One cannot consume vampire media and not know of Dracula at this point, even if many vampire lovers haven't read the original novel. The vampires we think of now are often derived from Bram Stoker's *Dracula* rather than ancient myths or the lore that inspired the novel. New creators tweak Dracula's rules (e.g., some can't go out into the sun while others sparkle in it), but they are essentially playing telephone with vampire lore as they create new stories around the enthralling themes of Stoker's work.

Predominantly, *Dracula* and *Carmilla* (see page 144,) initiated the cultural connection between themes of sexuality and vampirism. Stoker's *Dracula* (and other Draculas that follow) link the forbidden hunger for blood that vampires experience with sexual desire. For audiences at the time of publication, readers were likely meant to link the sexual deviancy of Dracula and his brides as a sign of just how evil, immoral, and against the Church these creatures were. For modern audiences, there are background themes of shame and "wanting something you shouldn't," which may align with Stoker potentially being romantically interested in men at a time when anti-homosexuality laws made that a crime.

While there are a slew of other strong themes in the book that play out in modern vampire stories (themes of power and what charm and political clout can mask; validating xenophobia and fear of the unknown; the line between magic and the supernatural), the largest cultural impact Stoker's work had was transforming the slowly decomposing undead vampires of

MINI DRACULA DIRECTORY

Dracula is a prolific character in the media, and listing all his appearances would be an extensive project that would constantly find itself in need of an update. What follows are some of his most iconic representations.

Bram Stoker's novel (1897): The original Dracula and certainly the most mysterious.

Max Shreck in *Nosferatu* (1922): An unlicensed German adaptation with nearly an identical plot that only altered the name from Count Dracula to Count Orlok. The adaptation was considered copyright infringement by Stoker's estate and most copies were destroyed.

Bela Lugosi, directed by Tod Browning (1931): An iconic performance from Bela Lugosi solidified this interpretation of Dracula as canon. The traits the character is known for—pale skin, inflections and accents, inky black hair with a widow's peak, sweeping cape, and charming yet creepy presence—are often replicated from Lugosi's portrayal.

Gary Oldman, directed by Francis Ford Coppola (1992): This version took steps to explain Dracula's origins and provided a more empathetic portrayal of the man behind the monster.

Eastern Europe into attractive and affluent immortals. They are no longer small-town peasants menacing their family and friends from beyond the grave until their corpse is burned. Thanks to Dracula, vampires' mythology became untethered from the roots of their folklore. If pop culture is to be believed, vampires are hungrier for something more than small-town fare.

THE VAMPIRE CHRONICLES AND *INTERVIEW WITH THE VAMPIRE* BY ANNE RICE (1976)

The first book in Anne Rice's most popular novel series, The Vampire Chronicles, was the 1976 *Interview with the Vampire*, which kicked off a pop-culture vampiric mainstay for more than fifty years. Rice wrote thirteen books in the series to expand upon vampire lore from the original book.

The first novel was adapted for film in 1994 with Hollywood A-listers Brad Pitt and Tom Cruise, along with Kirsten Dunst in her first major film role. So poignant was the cultural phenomenon that a prestige television series began airing in 2022, with the same characters telling a more modern version of the story as adapted by the author's son, Christopher Rice.

The Vampire Chronicles as a series focuses on the vampire Lestat de Lioncourt, but *Interview with the Vampire* is a story told in the first person from a New Orleans vampire named Louis de Pointe du Lac. Louis laments the horrors and agony of being a vampire in an interview with a plucky reporter. Throughout his story, his complex relationships with Lestat de Lioncourt (the vampire that made him) and Claudia (their immortal vampire child) serve as a driving force for the novel.

Folklore Sources Referenced

Rice uses Stoker's Dracula as a model for her vampires in The Vampire Chronicles. They need blood to live, sleep in coffins, and cannot go out in the sun. There are a few pieces of folklore that are referenced in *Interview with the Vampire*, but it's unclear whether this is done intentionally. For example, when the freshly turned vampire Louis and his maker Lestat travel to New Orleans, news travels of a mysterious plague ripping through the slums as Lestat feeds on humans. This wasting illness is quite like the illnesses that inspired rural towns of the 1700s to believe their dead were returning to dredge life from the living.

Cultural Context

As previously highlighted by the main relationship in *Carmilla* and the undertones in *Dracula*, vampires have historically been queer-coded in fiction. The relationship between Lestat and Louis was no different, and was perceived by fans to be romantic in nature. Not only does Lestat's obsession with making Louis his companion appear more romantic than friendly, but also a large section of the book revolves around their vampire family, which is composed of two men and the daughter they are raising together. This interpretation took off in online fan adaptations that portrayed Louis and Lestat as lovers and led to Rice becoming litigious about unlicensed, unmonetized fan works of her characters. Through gentle suggestions from her son Christopher, also a *New York Times* best-selling writer, Rice's initial qualms with the interpretation dissipated and the subsequent 2022 television series, also called *Interview with the Vampire*, leans into the romantic (albeit toxic) relationship between Lestat and Louis.

Additionally, Rice's Southern Gothic vampire novel was essentially the *Dracula* of the twentieth century. It brought writing about vampires, which was at the time a fringe goth subculture, back into critical acclaim. She also portrayed the first "good guy" vampire, one that struggled with his morality and could sustain himself on animal blood rather than human blood. Rice's themes surrounding the dichotomies of life and death, morality and nihilism, and isolation and community gave critics and fans a lot to chew on and launched vampires into the mainstream.

VAMPIRE: THE MASQUERADE (1991)

Although *Vampire: The Masquerade* (*VtM*) is a tabletop role-playing game like *Dungeons & Dragons*, the similarities end there. *Vampire: The Masquerade* took the game market by storm upon its release in 1991, presenting an urban horror landscape populated by vampires wrestling with morality, clan politics, and unending hunger. Players take on the role of vampires living in the modern era, each with special powers (and weaknesses) corresponding to the vampire clan that they were brought into when they were bitten. Each player decides for themselves what their character is like and how they fit into the wider vampire society, then role-play with friends (led by a "Storyteller") to tell a collaborative story.

As *Vampire: The Masquerade* took off, its creators began work on companion games telling the story of other supernatural creatures in the same world. Games like *Werewolf: The Apocalypse*, *Mage: The Ascension*, and *Changeling: The Lost* became part of the shared universe known as the *World of Darkness*. By using the same basic rules in each game, the designers made it possible for players to combine them for their own stories, allowing for vampires, werewolves, mages, and more to share the table. Subsequent editions of *World of Darkness* took a more international approach to storytelling, incorporating folklore from different countries and setting stories in cities in different countries.

Folklore Sources Referenced

The vampires in *Vampire: The Masquerade* have some traits that reflect what we see in traditional vampire tales. Vampires are undead, transformed by being drained of blood by a vampire and then receiving the vampire's blood in return. This is similar to the

concerns found in Eastern Europe in the eighteenth and nineteenth centuries that a person could be turned into a vampire by coming into contact with vampire blood. *Vampire: The Masquerade* adds a twist to the idea that vampires are repelled by crucifixes; any item that represents a human's "faith" can repel a vampire, even if their faith is capitalism and the item is a credit card!

In *Vampire: The Masquerade*, a vampire's clan decides what special powers they possess. The Toreador are seductive, the Tremere are magicians, and the Gangrel are shapeshifters, for example. Each of these clans draws its inspiration from different types of vampire folklore, including many examples covered in this book. All vampires in the *World of Darkness* are descendants of Cain, their immortality stemming from the curse he received from God; this has been a common theory about vampires' origins from the medieval era to today.

Cultural Context

In the 1990s, *Vampire: The Masquerade* helped fan the flames of the vampire renaissance happening in pop culture. It opened up a market for both tabletop and live-action role-playing that found huge popularity in the goth and punk communities, subcultures that had not had a large presence in gaming up to that point. The release of video game adaptations like *Vampire: The Masquerade–Bloodlines* further cemented the game's notoriety, and introduced characters like Jeannette Voerman, a vampire nightclub owner with a split personality. *Vampire: The Masquerade* helped popularize a number of modern vampire tropes, such as the rivalry between vampires and werewolves and the idea of a vampire "prince" who rules a given city or area of territory. While its influence on later works is clear, the game's creators sometimes took issue with what they saw as copyright infringement.

The fifth edition of *Vampire: The Masquerade* was published in 2018, creating a resurgence of interest in the property. Just as Dungeons & Dragons saw new players pour in thanks to online live play shows like *Critical Role*, the *Vampire: The Masquerade* live show *L.A. By Night*, and its sequel *N.Y. By Night*, brought a whole new generation of fans to the game. Through more than twenty years and five editions, *Vampire: The Masquerade* continues to encourage everyone to tell their own vampire stories.

VAMPIRE ACTION

Vampires were all the rage in film and television in the 1990s, leading to their appearance in several different genres. Action stories were particularly successful, especially when they incorporated unique twists to set themselves apart from previous horror films about vampires.

In 1992, *Buffy the Vampire Slayer* premiered, and subverted one of horror's most common tropes, the blonde cheerleader. Buffy, played by Sarah Michelle Gellar, inherited the powers of the Slayer and took up the fight against vampires and other evils. For seven seasons, *Buffy the Vampire Slayer* promoted teenage girls as action-adventure heroines and pulled audiences into the imperiled town of Sunnydale, California, where witches, demons, werewolves, and vampires ran wild. The show owes its concept to the 1992 film version, starring

Kristy Swanson as Buffy. A spin-off, called *Angel*, premiered in 1999, focusing on the titular vampire (who was Buffy's love interest in *Buffy the Vampire Slayer*) starting a detective agency in Los Angeles to fight the evil law firm Wolfram & Hart, with the backing of the heavenly Powers that Be. *Buffy the Vampire Slayer* and *Angel* used their modern California setting to present heroes dealing with a blend of supernatural and mundane challenges, helping to popularize fantasy and horror elements in mainstream television.

Another classic vampire hunter of modern media is Blade, who premiered in Marvel comics in 1973 before being launched onto the big screen in 1998. Blade (real name Eric Brooks) is a dhampir (see page 120), blessed with many vampire powers but immune to daylight, which makes him an ideal vampire hunter. He contends with an urban infestation of vampires both ancient and new, who often scheme to use magical rituals to increase their power and prey on the human

world. Actor Wesley Snipes's performance as Blade has become a cult classic role, leading to several film sequels. Today, Blade is poised to return to film in an upcoming reboot from Marvel Studios, and he's now the proud father of a daughter named Brielle in the comics (who also hunts vampires).

Kate Beckinsale first appeared as the vampire Selene in the movie *Underworld* in 2003, spawning a long-lasting film franchise following the ongoing war between vampires and werewolves, called "lycans" in the movie series. The stylish goth aesthetic and blood-pumping action of the film made it a box-office hit, and it further popularized the vampire-werewolf rivalry seen earlier in *Vampire: The Masquerade*, and later in the Twilight Saga and *True Blood*. An example of the "good vampire" trope discussed earlier (see page 156), Selene was a vampire protagonist trying to do the right thing in a morally messy world, though her feminine leather-clad look likely owes something to Buffy and Blade as well. Audiences were hooked by the intricate backstory afforded to *Underworld*'s vampires and lycans, who share an ancient connection that has fueled their conflict.

Folklore Sources Referenced

Buffy's vampires are said to be both undead and demonic; any humans who are bitten die (with the soul passing on to the afterlife), while the body is possessed by a demon who adopts that human's personality and memories. The show often references ancient mythology (some of it real, some of it made up) in support of its storylines. Buffy does most of her vampire slaying by staking or beheading vampires, with sunlight, fire, crosses, and holy water also appearing in her arsenal.

Blade is a rare example of a dhampir in modern vampire media, though unlike his folkloric inspirations, his father is not a vampire. Blade's mother was bitten by a vampire while pregnant and managed to give birth before dying of blood loss; Blade's exposure to the vampire's bite while in the womb gave him some vampiric powers, but shielded him from the vampire's weaknesses. In his earliest appearances, Blade used teakwood knives to fight vampires, a unique addition by the author.

Underworld's vampires and lycans are revealed to share a common ancestor, making them distant cousins. This seems fitting given the ambiguity and overlap between vampires and werewolves in some folklore. In Balkan countries like Greece and Serbia, werewolves and vampires often had very similar powers, and were sometimes attested to be the same creature.

Cultural Context

Buffy the Vampire Slayer and *Blade* helped move the age-old conflict between vampire and vampire hunter from the realm of medieval fantasy to a contemporary urban setting, cementing the pop-cultural image of vampires lurking in nightclubs and alleyways. Vampires weren't just the stuff of horror films and Gothic literature anymore, but could hold their own in the kind of action stories that appealed to a broad demographic. *Buffy's* romance and drama elements (particularly the doomed love between Buffy and Angel) also helped pave the way for later series that centered on vampire romances with Byronic love interests.

With Blade poised to return to cinemas, and the prospect of more *Underworld* movies in the future, vampire action films seem unlikely to disappear anytime soon. Meanwhile, the world of Buffy is still growing nearly thirty years on, with spin-off comics, novels, and audio dramas that continue the stories of the Slayers for a new generation.

VAMPIRE ROMANCE

Following the mainstream success of the vampire action movies in the 1990s and early 2000s came a wave of vampire romances that further solidified the cultural opinion that "good" vampires make excellent romantic heroes. In the 2000s and early aughts, bloody epic vampire romances reigned supreme with audiences of young women, and there are three breakout successes.

Spanning nearly as much time in cultural relevance as *Buffy*, the first Vampire Diaries young adult book, *The Awakening* by L. J. Smith, was published in 1991 when YA was an emerging genre, and the most recent addition of the thirteen-book series (ghostwritten by Aubrey Clark) hit the shelves in 2017. The premise follows high-school student Elena Gilbert as she falls in love with a handsome new kid named Stefan Salvatore (secretly a one-hundred-plus-year-old vampire sworn off human blood matriculating in his former hometown) amidst a spree of brutal murders believed to be carried out by Stefan's older, more bloodthirsty vampire brother, Damon Salvatore. The book series regained popularity in 2009 when television network The CW aired *The Vampire Diaries* series starring Nina Dobrev as Elena and heartthrobs Paul Wesley and Ian Somerhalder— Stefan, and Damon, respectively—playing the main characters in a sordid love triangle between Elena and the Salvatore brothers. Public adoration has carried the TV series through two spin-off series called *The Originals* (2013–2018) and *Legacies* (2018–2022). The television series and later books build on a world of vampire hunters, witches, and werewolves in a way that is reminiscent of *Vampire: The Masquerade*.

Mimicking the success, premise, and general trajectory of The Vampire Diaries, the Twilight Saga (published 2005–2008) follows the life another teenage heroine,

Bella Swan, when she moves to Forks, Washington, and meets a classmate at her new school, Edward Cullen, who is secretly a mind-reading vampire sworn off feeding on humans. The series follows the couple's romance, while also building out vampire society and shapeshifters that live unbeknownst to humans. One such shapeshifter is Jacob Black, who vies for Bella's affections. It culminates with Bella and Edward getting married, having a half-vampire-half-human daughter, and Bella turning into a vampire. The book series was a near immediate hit resulting in a movie franchise (2008–2012) starring Kristen Stewart as Bella, Robert Pattinson as Edward, and Taylor Lautner as Jacob.

The Southern Vampire Mysteries series by Charlaine Harris spanned three novels (published 2001–2013) and television network HBO aired eight seasons of the TV drama adaptation, *True Blood* (2008–2014). Set in the fictional town of Bon Temps, Louisiana, both series are set after a synthetic version of blood called True Blood allows vampires to "come out of the coffin" and live among humans in the open. The show's main character, a psychic waitress named Sookie Stackhouse (played by Anna Paquin), solves murders and falls

in love with vampires (most notably vampires Bill Compton and Eric Northman, played by Stephen Moyer and Alexander Skarsgård, respectively), werewolves, shape shifters, and fay creatures throughout the series. The show (primarily written by showrunner Alan Ball) was beloved by fans and critics alike and won a Golden Globe and an Emmy.

Folklore Sources Referenced

The authors in these cases pull from well-known vampire mythology of the modern audiences, which is almost entirely derived from previous works of fiction such as *Dracula*, *Buffy*, and *Vampire: The Masquerade*.

Vampires in The Vampire Diaries are weakened by an herb called vervain, which has medicinal properties but was rarely associated with protection from vampires. Some more powerful vampires can only be killed with a white oak stake, which differs from the traditional hawthorn. Interestingly, like *Vampire: The Masquerade* and the vrykolaka, vampires and werewolves share a common ancestor and can create hybrids, like the dhampir, but their ties to the folklore of both are loose at best.

Vampires in the Twilight Saga famously don't burst into flames in the sunlight, but rather sparkle. The series also leans toward decapitation as the primary method of eliminating a vampire, and the series' vampires all have unique powers, some of which align with the vampires of folklore and others that probably just seemed cool to the author. The vampire hybrid again harkens to the dhampir, but Bella and Edward's daughter, Renesmee, is said to live an immortal life rather than a brief one consisting of killing vampires.

True Blood vampires align the closest to the vampires of folklore—they sleep in coffins, die by being staked, have heightened senses, and are superfast and strong. Later seasons of the television show fold in the mythology of the ancient vampire Lilith (see page 126).

While the genre of paranormal romance also softens the folklore that these creatures are steeped in disease and horror, there is something to be said about the inherently sexual aspects of vampires in mythology. Many of the vampires in folklore return to their wives in death and have sexual relations with them. Reports from victims of Peter Plogojowitz (see page 99) stated that he attacked them ithyphallic (or, in other words, with an erection). This is likely due to the release of gases during the decomposition process, but it still stands true that many versions of the medieval vampire are as sexually active as the ones in modern paranormal romances.

Cultural Context

There are countless vampire romances in the media at this point, but these three in the 2000s and early 2010s are what launched and perfected the genre. As vampires in fiction began as romantic creatures, it seems only fair that they too get to feel the love in the developed versions of their stories. The Vampire Diaries has actually been in the cultural zeitgeist for as long as *Buffy*, although the series receives less critical acclaim. This is likely due to many different reasons, but could potentially be because when something is made almost exclusively with a feminine audience in mind, its work is seen as a bit more derivative and less impactful. The same can be said for both

Twilight Saga and *True Blood*, which are wildly popular but more vocally criticized (likely by people outside of the audience that know it best and enjoy it).

While the Twilight Saga and *The Vampire Diaries* were both normative in regard to the stories they were telling, *True Blood* boasted a diverse ensemble cast, slasher-style levels of gore, and LGBTQ+ representation, driving storylines with gritty themes, witty banter, and graphic sex scenes. Once one vampire romance successfully incorporated these themes, others began to as well. The 2022 television series *Interview with the Vampire* not only explicitly stated that characters were queer, but also repositioned Louis from a beloved plantation owner in Louisiana (which is cringeworthy to look at in the 2020s) in the original novel and 1994 film adaptation to a Black business owner facing the racism of Louisiana in the 1910s.

It's easy to look at vampires now and think that these creatures of the night have developed into being only an object for teenage girls' affections, but these works are influential to popular culture in positive ways. It is reductive to view vampire romances as exclusively derivative while viewing their predecessors as classics, especially when they continue to change what it means to be a fictional vampire in ways that matter to real humans.

Conclusion

Preternatural sciences (or the study of miraculous and macabre things, such as vampires) was a legitimate science by doctors, physicists, and engineers (at least) up until as late as the 1920s. As radio waves and radiation were being discovered, scientists and skeptics were able to believe in invisible waves of sound and energy that were imperceptible to humans but nonetheless something real that could be manipulated. Likewise, believing in the unbelievable—like vampires, witches, cryptids, and ghosts—with a healthy dose of skepticism and curiosity was nearly a scientific endeavor.

The vampire mania that engulfed Europe in the 1800s is easy enough to explain with modern medical science, but just because a few cases are easily disprovable doesn't mean the supernatural doesn't exist somewhere. We only know of black holes because of the absence of light—they devour the light like a celestial vampire.

As is their nature, vampires will likely continue to haunt our stories. They are the call of the void after death and a walking chance at redemption. Their place as a monster in our stories will help us continue to redefine what it means to be human. Folklore and fiction are meant to tell us more about ourselves than the monsters they warn us about.

Still . . . it couldn't hurt to hang garlic from your porch, treat the spirits of your dearly departed kindly, and sing songs to your hearth to protect your home at night.

Acknowledgments

Vampires have always been deeply fascinating to me, and I'd like to thank Cara Donaldson for helping me climb into this coffin and editor Elizabeth You for helping me give this book life. Much gratitude to the libraries that carry a robust collection of creepy books used to fact check folklore. I'd like to thank my friends and loved ones who pretended to be interested when I brought up another weird vampire that they simply *had* to know about.

Finally, I'd like to thank sixteen-year-old-me, who couldn't get enough of vampires and would be delighted to know that we literally wrote the book on them.

About the Author

Agnes Hollyhock is a lifelong lover of cryptids who lives in a mildly haunted house in Massachusetts. Along with the ghosts, she lives with her beloved animal companions, a cat named Jack and a tarantula named Sally.

Resources and References

Bane, Theresa. *Encyclopedia of Vampire Mythology*, McFarland & Company, Incorporated Publishers, 2010.

Barber, Paul. *Vampires, Burial, and Death: Folklore and Reality*, Yale University Press, 1988.

Dundes, Alan. *The Vampire: A Casebook*, University of Wisconsin Press, 1998.

Groom, Nick. *The Vampire: A New History*, Yale University Press, 2018.

Konstantinos. *Vampires: The Occult Truth*. Llewellyn, 1996.

McClelland, Bruce A. *Slayers and Their Vampires: A Cultural History of Killing the Dead*, University of Michigan Press, 2006.

Melton, J. Gordon and Alysa Hornick, compilers. *The Vampire in Folklore, History, Literature, Film and Television: A Comprehensive Bibliography*, McFarland & Company, Inc., Publishers, 2015.

Murgatroyd, Paul. *Mythical Monsters in Classical Literature*, Bloomsbury Publishing, 2007.

Index

First published in 2024 by Wellfleet Press,
an imprint of The Quarto Group,
142 West 36th Street, 4th Floor,
New York, NY 10018, USA
(212) 779-4972
www.Quarto.com

Wellfleet Press titles are also available at discount for retail, wholesale, promotional, and bulk purchase. For
details, contact the Special Sales Manager by email at specialsales@quarto.com or by mail at The Quarto
Group, Attn: Special Sales Manager, 100 Cummings Center Suite 265D, Beverly, MA 01915 USA.

10 9 8 7 6 5 4 3 2

ISBN: 978-1-57715-446-4

Digital edition published in 2024
eISBN: 978-0-7603-9024-5

Library of Congress Cataloging-in-Publication Data

Names: Hollyhock, Agnes, author.
Title: Vampires : a handbook of the history & lore of the undead / Agnes Hollyhock.
Description: New York, NY : Wellfleet Press, 2024. | Includes
    bibliographical references and index. | Summary: "Vampires is your
    beautifully illustrated mystical guide to the undead and their lore
    throughout the centuries"-- Provided by publisher.
Identifiers: LCCN 2024000451 (print) | LCCN 2024000452 (ebook) | ISBN
    9781577154464 (hardcover) | ISBN 9780760390245 (ebook)
Subjects: LCSH: Vampires--History. | Vampires--Folklore.
Classification: LCC GR830.V3 H65 2024 (print) | LCC GR830.V3 (ebook) |
    DDC 398.21--dc23/eng/202402007
LC record available at https://lccn.loc.gov/2024000451
LC ebook record available at https://lccn.loc.gov/2024000452

Group Publisher: Rage Kindelsperger
Editorial Director: Erin Canning
Creative Director: Laura Drew
Senior Art Director: Marisa Kwek
Managing Editor: Cara Donaldson
Editor: Elizabeth You
Cover Design: Marisa Kwek
Interior Design: Raine Rath
Interior Illustrations by Raine Rath: 4, 6, 9, 10, 12, 21, 28, 50, 56, 90,
94, 105, 108, 114, 116, 132, 135, 140, 154, 161, 170

Printed in China